The Uttermost Star

...and Other Gleams of Fancy

By Frank W. Boreham

PANTIANOS
CLASSICS

Published by Pantianos Classics

ISBN-13: 978-1-78987-320-7

First published in 1919

Contents

By Way of Introduction

An author putting the finishing touches to his manuscript and writing his Introduction resembles a hostess preparing to receive her guests. For weeks she has been engaged in making the most careful preparations for their entertainment. Now the evening has arrived; her great hour has come; she is about to take up her position at the door. Her anxious eye wanders restlessly over the polished floors, the pictured walls, the cosy chairs, the faultless tables — everything. She sees that every flower is showing to the best advantage; that every noble vase and marble statuette is in its place; and that every lamp is casting its softest, loveliest glow.

But what is that? The sound of wheels! They draw up at the gate! Throw the doors wide open! The first guests are arriving!

Welcome! a thousand welcomes! If those who accept the hospitality of these pages find in them half the pleasure that their preparation has afforded me, I shall count myself the happiest of hosts.

Frank W. Boreham.

Armadale, Melbourne, Australia,
 Easter, 1919.

Part One

I - The Signal-Box

When I was a small boy in my Kentish home, I was occasionally missing — even at meal-times. As the years wore on, the alarm created by these mysterious disappearances of mine gradually subsided, not by reason of any dwindling value or importance attached to my person, but simply because a very shrewd conjecture could be formed as to my whereabouts. For at the foot of our garden, separated from it by a high bank, which was itself a romantic wilderness of blackberries, ran the railway. And just beside the railway line, not more than a hundred yards from the bottom of the garden, was the signalbox. Few things delighted me more than to spend an hour in that old signal-box. It was close to the mouth of the tunnel. I loved to hear the bell go ring-a-ting-ting when the train entered the tunnel on the far side, and to watch for its emergence on our side. It seemed to me positively uncanny that the signalman could tell by all these clanging tokens just where all the trains were. I liked to see him swing the great levers backwards and forwards, pulling the signals up and down, and at night-time causing the green and red lights to shine from the tall signal-posts. As I sat beside his great roaring fire on winter evenings, and saw him stop the trains or let them pass, just as he pleased, I thought he must surely be one of the most important men in the country. I could scarcely imagine that the Prime Minister had greater authority or responsibility. And I remember, as clearly as though it were yesterday, that I used to sit on the stool beside that fire — face in hands and elbows on knees — wondering if I might hope, one great day, to attain to the glory of being a signalman. And, surely enough, I have!

For I have come to see, as the days have gone by, that we humans are expert and inveterate signalmen. We have a perfect genius for concocting mysterious codes; we revel in flashing out cryptic heliograms; we glory in receiving occult messages. We even communicate in this abstruse and recondite fashion with our own selves. A man will twist a piece of string round his finger, or tie a knot in the corner of his pocket-handkerchief, or stick a scrap of stamp-paper on the face of his watch, to remind him of something that has nothing whatever to do with string or handkerchief or stamp-paper. It is his secret code, and in the terms of that code this inveterate signalman is signalling to himself, that is all!

Moreover, we not only signal to ourselves, but we are fascinated by the spectacle of other people signalling to themselves. A novel becomes invested with a new interest when its plot suddenly turns upon the weird phenomena of a witch's cavern or the mysterious ritual of a gipsy camp. By means of her viper, her owl, her toad, her cauldron, her tripod, her herbs, and all the rest of it, the withered crone in the dimly lighted cave is signalling to herself from morning to night; by means of the crossed sticks where the roads fork the gipsies leave tokens for themselves and each other. Many a man will wear a charm hanging round his neck, or suspended to his watch-chain, of which nobody knows the significance but himself. Luther went down to his grave without revealing even to his wife the meaning of the five mystic initials that he had carved over the portal of his house. They are, he explained, the initials of five German words; but what those words were he alone knew. The signals stand to this day over the portal; the code was locked up in the great reformer's breast, and, deposited there, it descended with him to his tomb.

Henrik Ibsen, too, the great Norwegian dramatist, kept on his writing-table a small ivory tray containing a number of grotesque figures, a wooden bear, a tiny devil, two or three cats — one of them playing a fiddle — and some rabbits. I never write a single line of any of my dramas,' Ibsen used to say, 'without having that tray and its occupants before me on my table. I could not write without them. But why I use them and how, this is my own secret.' Here was a great and brilliant thinker happy in being able to flash covert messages to himself by a code which no one but himself ever knew! I instance these — the witch's cavern, the gipsy's ritual, the reformer's portal, and the dramatist's tray — to show that our passion for signalling is so ingrained and deep-seated that, if we cannot satisfy it in cryptic communication with others, we atone for the deficiency by signalling to ourselves.

After all, there is but one really universal language. It was spoken in the world's first morning, and men will still be speaking it when they are startled by the shocks of doom. It was the language of the Stone Age, and it will be the language of the Golden Age. It is spoken all the world over by men of all kinds, classes, colours, and conditions; and if either Mars or the moon is really inhabited, it is spoken there too. The little child speaks it before he is able to lisp one single word of our clumsier dictionary speech; and the aged speak it long after the palsied lip has lost its utterance. It is equally intelligible to the English merchant on the London market, to the Indian trapper in the Western forests, to the Chinese mandarin in the far interior of Asia, to the South Sea Islander basking in the rays of an equatorial sun, and to the Eskimo in his frozen hut amidst the blinding whiteness of the icy North. It is known even to the beasts of the field and the birds of the air; they understand it, and sometimes even speak it. The universal language is the language of gesture. The shrug of the shoulders; the flash of the eye; the knitting of the brows; the curling of the lip; the stamping of the foot; the clenching of the fist; the nodding of the head; the pointing of the hand, — here is a language which is known to every one. It has no alphabet, no grammar, and no syntax; but the simplest can understand it. Indeed, the simplest understand it best. The savage is a master of gesture. He speaks with every nerve and muscle. And the little child is no less eloquent. Playing with her doll on the floor behind my chair is a small scrap of humanity who has as yet uttered no word that a lexicographer would recognize. And yet it would be absurd to say that she has not spoken. Her pushings and pullings, her beckonings and pointings, her smilings and poutings, are as expressive as anything in any of your vocabularies. She has found a speech for which the builders of Babel sighed in vain — a speech that can be understood by men and women of every nation under heaven. It is the language of signals.

We are living in a universe that is constantly trying to talk. It does not understand any of your artificial or manufactured languages — your Hebrew or Greek or Latin; your English or German or French — but it understands the universal language, the language of gestures, the language of signals. 'The air,' says Emerson, 'is full of sounds, the sky of tokens; the ground is all memoranda and signatures; and every object is covered over with hints which speak to the intelligent.' The stars above my head are signalling; the astronomer masters the code and reads the secrets of the universe. The stones that I tread beneath my feet are signalling; the geologist unravels the code and interprets the romance of ages.

All Nature is one intricate system of signals, as any naturalist will tell you. Let Richard Jefferies speak for them all. In discussing the birds that shelter in the ivy under his gable, he says that often a robin or a wren will pounce upon a caterpillar whilst the grub is still concealed among the grass. How is it done? It is all a matter of signals. 'The bird's eyes, ever on the watch for food, learn to detect the slightest indication of its presence. Slugs, caterpillars, and such creatures, in moving among the grass, cause a slight agitation of the grass blades; they lift up a leaf by crawling under it, or depress it with their weight by getting on it. This enables the bird to detect their presence, even when quite hidden by the herbage, experience having taught it that, when grass is moved by the wind, broad patches sway simultaneously, whilst, when an insect or caterpillar is the agent, only a single leaf or blade is stirred.' The birds learn the code and readily interpret the signals. Those who live near to Nature soon acquire the same habit. The poetry of the countryside abounds with rhymes and couplets that are, after all, only expositions of Nature's signals.

When elm leaves are as big as a shilling,
You may sow French beans if you be willing.

What is this but the interpretation of the code? The whispering elm leaves are the farmer's signal-flags. The universe, like the baby on my study floor, is always pathetically trying to talk to me; and the pity of it is that I am so slow to understand.

The language of signals is, I have shown, the one universal language. That is why, when man has something really great to say, he says it, not audibly, but visibly. The lover abandons the dictionary; he can say what he wishes to say so much more expressively by means of signals, A look; a pressure of the hand; a ring; a kiss, — what vocabulary could compare with a code like this?

And it is a code that is comprehended in every nation under heaven. Or what man could express in so many words all that he feels, when, for example, he waves his country's flag? 'Have not I,' Carlyle makes Herr Teufelsdrockh inquire, 'have not I myself known five hundred living soldiers sabred into crow's meat for a piece of glazed cotton which they call their Flag; which, had you sold it at any market-cross, would not have brought above three groschen? Did not the whole Hungarian nation rise, like some tumultuous moon-stirred Atlantic, when Kaiser Joseph pocketed their Iron Crown, an implement, as was sagaciously observed, in size and commercial value little differing from a horseshoe? It is in and through symbols that man, consciously or unconsciously, lives, works, and has his being; those ages, moreover, are accounted the noblest which can the best recognize symbolic worth and prize it the highest. For is not a symbol ever, to him who has eyes for it, some dimmer or clearer revelation of the Godlike?' When, that is to say, man has something really great to say he says it by some mute sign or silent symbol. Similarly, when God has something to say to the Jew alone. He may perhaps cause His messenger to say it in the Hebrew tongue; but when He has something to say to all men everywhere, He always speaks the universal language, the language of gesture and symbol and sign. He speaks to the universal heart by means of the Ark, the Scapegoat, the Passover, the Mercy Seat, the Serpent in the Wilderness, the Cities of Refuge. Such signs need no translation; they speak to men of every clime and time. In the New Testament the same principle holds true.

He talked of lilies, vines, and corn,
    The sparrow and the raven,
And tales so natural, yet so wise,
    Were on men's hearts engraven.
And yeast and bread and flax and cloth,
    And eggs and fish and candles;
See, how the whole familiar world
    He most divinely handles.

When God has something really vital to say to man. He says it in a language that requires no translation or interpretation. He says it in a way that all men can comprehend. 'The veil of the temple was rent in twain from the top to the bottom.' All men everywhere can see the awful and profound significance of such a signal. A man may be unable to grasp the doctrine of the Atonement; but where is the heart that does not respond to the Vision of the Cross?

We are inveterate signalmen. We begin to make signals as soon as we crawl from our cradles; we are still making them when tottering down to our graves.

'It may be, master,' said Richard Bannatyne, John Knox's faithful serving-man, 'it may be that you will still be able to recognize my voice after you have become oblivious to every other sight and sound. When you are apparently unconscious, I shall bend over you and ask if you have still the hope of glory. Will you promise, if you are able to give me some signal, that you will do so?'

The old reformer made the promise, and, a few days later, turned into his room to die.

Grim in his deep death-anguish the stern old champion lay,
And the locks upon his pillow were floating thin and grey,
And, visionless and voiceless, with quick and labouring breath,
He waited for his exit through life's dark portal, death.

'Hast thou the hope of glory?' They bowed to catch the thrill
That through some languid token might be responsive still,
Nor watched they long nor waited for some obscure reply.
He raised a clay-cold finger and pointed to the sky.

So the death-angel found him, what time his brow he bent,
To give the struggling spirit a sweet enfranchisement.
So the death-angel left him, what time earth's bonds were riven,
The cold, stark, stiffening finger still pointing up to heaven.

It is a great thing when the signalman's last signals are as unequivocal as that.

II - The Uttermost Star

I HAVE been on a visit to the uttermost star. You will search all your learned astronomical volumes in vain for any reference to such a sphere. No observatory has descried it; it never swam into the field of even the most powerful telescope. The fact is that I discovered it myself. I was longing one day for a bird's-eye view of the universe. You do not get a satisfactory conception of the architecture of a cathedral by attending evening worship. You must see the glorious structure in the daytime and from a distance. Similarly, you do not know the universe till you have seen it from afar. You cannot see things in their right perspective. A sparrow on a housetop looks as big as a star in the sky. 'If,' I said to myself that morning, 'if only I could get right away from all the worlds, and if only I could view the universe from some point out beyond the universe, I should be able to compile a new standard of values. The little things that seem large because they are so near at hand will all vanish, and I shall know what those things are that still stand bravely out when everything else is lost in the infinite distance.'

And so I set out on my breathless flight. I cannot tell you how far I went. In a second or two I lost sight of the houses and the trees; in another I could no longer distinguish between the mountains and the plains. When next I glanced over my shoulder, the sea and the dry land were all as one. I could not tell where the one ended and the other began. And a moment later I had some difficulty in identifying the earth at all. I left the sun and the moon behind me before I paused for the first time; and I paused many and many a time before I reached my journey's end. At last the space before me was one vast unbroken void. All the whirling globes were circling behind me. I went on and on, day after day, through nothing but one boundless and terrific wilderness of solitude.

And then, just as I was thinking of taking my observations and returning, I found a new world! It was a lonely little world, a kind of astral outpost; the Ultima Thule of all the stellar systems. There it hung, poised in space, on the fringe of a vacant infinity! And there I paused. From the shores of this prodigal planet I surveyed the distant universe. There was something weirdly fantastic in seeing that universe, not as my dwelling-place enfolding me, but as a remote object on a far horizon. And what could I see of it? What were the things that stood clearly out, now that all the details were obscured? Of all the myriad objects that confused my sight when I dwelt upon the earth, I could now see clearly only two things.

I had a vision of wondrous *harmony!* All things kept their course in perfect and glorious unity. There was no clash, no confusion, no discord anywhere. This, surely, was what the patriarch meant when he said that *the morning stars sang together!* This, surely, was what the poet meant when he wrote of *the music of the spheres!* Out here, on the shores of the uttermost star, I was listening to the melodies of the universe; the song of the morning stars; the music of the spheres!

And I had a vision of wondrous *light!* The only other thing that I could see was that the universe was luminous. Some of the worlds, I had noticed in passing, were blazing in appalling splendours of their own; others were dead and cold, yet reflecting in their very barrenness the fierce glare that fell upon them from their brilliant neighbours. But at this distance I could not distinguish between the worlds that shone with a borrowed radiance and those that flamed with a lustre of their own. All that I could see was that the universe was all alight. Every world twinkled, glittered, burned, and shone!

Harmony — perfect, ceaseless, unbroken!

Light — soft, resplendent, beautiful!

These were the only things that were still discernible as I surveyed the universe from this lonely outpost. These, therefore, are the two greatest things upon it.

II

I have been on a visit to the Orient. And one memorable afternoon, when the sky was a vault of cloudless blue and all the earth was fair, I found myself wandering aimlessly but joyously among the soft green Syrian hills. I sat down on the side of a grassy knoll and feasted my eyes on the quiet beauty of this idyllic scene. Not many yards below me a little stream flowed gently past the foot of the sloping hillside and meandered through the silent valley. There was no laughter in its waters; they moved slowly and peacefully on. Reeds and rushes grew plentifully along its banks. All at once I realized that I was not alone. I heard first the bleating of sheep, and then, a little later, human footsteps. A shepherd came round the curve of the knoll, sauntering slowly, with his flock following at his heels. He was leading them down through the green pastures to the still waters. He did not notice me; his attention seemed to be fastened on the reeds flourishing beside the stream. When he reached them he began to look about, examining them with a critical eye. One, a tall one, was bent, and drooped towards him. The sheep may have broken it in browsing there the day before; or perhaps a gust of wind had caught it. Anyway, it was broken. With a rough hand he snatched at it; looked it up and down disdainfully; doubled it at the point at which it was damaged before; and tossed it out on to the gently moving waters. Then he cut for himself another reed, a sturdier one, without flaw or fault of any kind. And as he led his flock gently along the banks of the stream, watching the poor broken reed floating away on the sluggish current, he worked away with deft and practised fingers, and out of the faultless reed he fashioned for himself a flute. And when it was finished he put it to his lips, and, lo, the sweet, clear music filled all that peaceful valley!

Harmony! It was a vision of *Harmony!*

When he paused to take breath and to look around upon his flock, I rose and approached him. Until then he had been unconscious of my presence. I sat sometimes talking with him and sometimes listening to the soft, sweet strains of his flute, until the approach of sunset reminded us that it was time to be moving. I walked with him up to the fold. The sheep appeared to resent my presence, and did not follow so closely at his heels as on their way down the valley earlier in the day. I watched him as he counted them and secured them for the night. And then he took me to his shepherd-hut some distance up the hillside. It was dusk by the time we reached it. He took down a lamp from the shelf and lit it. It was an odd little lamp, shaped like a tiny urn, and the wick protruded from the spout. It smoked horribly. He had gone to the back of the hut for some sticks with which to light his fire. When he returned and found the place reeking with the evil odour of the smoke, he was angry with the lamp, and, lighting another, he blew this one out and flung it unceremoniously back to the shelf. The second lamp burned beautifully; the fire blazed up; and all the room was bright.

Light! It was a vision of *Light!*

After awhile the shepherd walked with me up the valley to my temporary home. It was a glorious starlit night: such a night as only the Orient knows. I bade him good-night at the door; and we parted. He went back to his hut and to his fold. I, tired out, went straight to bed. And that night I dreamed.

I dreamed of the broken reed, crushed and crumpled in the shepherd's hands, that I had seen floating away on the stream.

And I dreamed of the lamp, the smoking lamp, extinguished so ruthlessly by the shepherd's hand, that I had seen thrown in disdain back to the shelf.

III

I have been on a visit to the Land of Long Ago. In a trice I crossed well-nigh thirty centuries. I found myself in old Jerusalem. And near the Beautiful Gate of the Temple I saw a crowd gathered together. And with wild, seraphic fire a prophet was addressing them. 'He is coming!' he cried. 'He is coming! The King is coming! The Redeemer is coming! The Messiah is coming! He shall not cry, nor lift up, nor cause His voice to be heard in the street. A bruised reed shall He not break, and the smoking lamp shall He not quench —'

I was so startled that I hurried back across the centuries and sat down in this quiet study of mine to think.

'A bruised reed shall He not break!' I thought of the reed, crumpled in the shepherd's hand, that I had seen floating on that Syrian stream.

'A smoking lamp shall He not quench!' I thought of the lamp tossed in contempt upon the shepherd's shelf.

What could it mean? What could it mean?

IV

And then I saw what it all meant. The *shepherd's* way is the easy way. He snatches at the bruised reed, crushes it, and tosses it away on to the moving waters. And he takes another that has never been bruised, and from it he draws his melodies. He flings the smoking lamp back to the shelf and takes a new and faultless one, and from it he gets the light that fills his home with brightness. Anybody could do that. But the *Good Shepherd* of whom the prophet speaks takes the hard way. With infinite pity and infinite patience He works away at the bruised reed until from it He woos the eternal harmonies. With infinite pity and infinite patience

He trims and cleans the smoking lamp until from it He draws the light that never was on sea or shore.

The bruised reed! The bruised reed represents the things that have never been of any use; the things that are marred in the making. From the bruised reed He gets His choicest harmony!

The smoking lamp! The smoking lamp represents the things that have been useful, but have lost the usefulness they had. Once luminous, they have become loathsome; once shining, they now smoke. From the smoking lamp He gets His clearest light!

From the bruised reed — *Harmony!*

From the smoking lamp — *Light!*

And *Harmony* and *Light,* as I saw from the shores of the uttermost star, are the two greatest things in the universe.

13

III - Picking Up the Pile Light

To passengers below — dressing in the cabins or breakfasting in the saloon — the measured and rhythmic throb of the engines was the only indication that the great ship was in motion. After a smooth and uneventful run across the Bass Straits, the *Loongana* was gliding swiftly across the broad, unruffled waters of Port Philip Bay. In an hour's time we confidently hoped to be greeting friends ashore. But just then, to our profound disappointment, the unexpected happened. Right ahead of us a long, low, leaden bank of fog lay languidly across the waters, blotting out all trace of land. The *Loongana* pushed her bows straight into it, and in a few minutes we could scarcely see the vessel's length in any direction. Clouds of grey, misty vapour drifted to and fro; and nothing was visible to us but a narrow circle of sea. The bells in the engine-room rang out sharply, communicating to the powerful turbines below the will of the officer high up on the bridge. The ship perceptibly slackened her pace. The bells rang out again, and the ship moved still more slowly. She simply crawled. Her loud and raucous syren proclaimed to all the craft in the vicinity her sure approach. Every few minutes great, ghostly ships, lying at anchor, sprang suddenly out of the mist. We were almost up to them before we saw their tall and shadowy masts looming spectrally above us. More ringing of bells, and the engines stopped altogether. Then, after a pause, we crept cautiously forward again, like a man groping his way in the dark. The apparitions that came suddenly upon us, and that as suddenly vanished again, were all of them the ghosts of things movable. From not one of them could we glean any sure knowledge as to our exact position. Here is a clumsy old dredge; there lies a tall ship riding at anchor; yonder is a snorting little motor-boat. But nothing fixed; nothing stable; nothing reliable. We are whelmed in uncertainty. A little later came the change which I have set out to describe; but at this stage we were enveloped in the haze and surrounded by objects from which our position could not with confidence be reckoned.

Such an experience has three perils. There is the danger of getting into shallow water and going aground; there is the danger of running down some other vessel; and there is the danger of being ourselves run down. All three of these disasters are fairly common. I fancy I have noticed that the people who get into the shallows of life, and become stranded there, are invariably people who were getting on very rapidly without being quite certain of their course. Although the horizon was by no means clear, and no fixed objects stood bravely out to guide them, they found a certain exhilaration in continuing at topmost speed. Unhappily, in such cases, the exhilaration does not last; there is nothing particularly exhilarating in being stuck in the mud! And, worse still, there is certainly nothing very exhilarating in being fast on a jagged reef! In either of these situations, a ship becomes a misery to herself and a menace to all the craft around her.

I remember, years ago, seeing the *Elginshire* hard and fast on the rocks on the east coast of New Zealand. She had been wrecked on her maiden trip. There she stood, a fine vessel, as erect as a ship in port! It seemed incredible that, looking so trim and taut, she was nevertheless wrecked beyond redemption. The New Zealand Government eventually ordered her to be blown up, lest other ships, seeing her lying there in apparent safety, should be decoyed by her to a similar fate. On the whole it is better to forfeit the exhilaration and to proceed slowly, with bells clanging and syrens screaming.

And then of course, there is the risk of a collision. It would be distinctly unpleasant to see, looming darkly out of the mist, and bearing down upon us, the gigantic proportions of some huge liner, several times as large as our own ship! It was thus that the *Empress of Ireland* perished in the fog on the St. Lawrence a few years ago. These deafening blasts on the syren are a contrivance for our own protection and for other people's. George MacDonald tells of a blind man who always carried a lantern. People used to ask him of what use the lantern could be to his sightless eyes. 'I do not carry it,' he replied, 'to prevent my stumbling over others, but to keep them from stumbling over me!' The man who, uncertain as to his course, goes calmly on, without in any way expressing his perplexity, is courting a most terrible disaster. By his very silence he may easily destroy his own ship — or somebody else's.

Yes, his own or somebody else's; and other people's ships are worth thinking about. Once, in my New Zealand days, I revisited England. Shall I ever forget the excitement of sighting the English coast and of anchoring in Plymouth Sound? We sent telegrams to the home folks, telling them the exact hour at which they might expect us next day. Then once more the great ship stood out to sea and began her voyage up the Channel. And, off the Nore, down came the fog! Down, too, to our unspeakable disgust, went the anchor! There we waited and waited and waited, half deafened by the screamings and hootings of the horns that answered to our own, and half blinded by the frantic efforts that we made to pierce the all-enshrouding mists and see the land near by! Presently the captain came sauntering along the deck, a picture of colossal calm.

'This is very exasperating,' I observed. 'We sent telegrams from Plymouth, telling the people at home when to meet us, and they'll be waiting at the docks now. Is there no possibility of getting on?'

'All very fine for you!' the skipper replied cheerily. 'You are on a ten-thousand ton liner. And you would like me to go on up the river, crumpling up everything we happen to strike as though it were made of brown paper! No, no; we've got the other ships to think of!'

To be sure! We have the other ships to think of. Many a time since, when the thick fogs have enveloped me, and I have been uncertain of my course, and have nevertheless been tempted to go full steam ahead, I have recalled the old sea captain's rebuke. There are others to think of.

But I spoke just now of the change that came later. It came quite suddenly. All at once the clamorous bells in the engine-room became busy again. The powerful turbines at the stern are once more churning the water into foam, and very soon a broad wake lies out behind the steamer. She is moving forward, not timorously, but with obvious confidence. What has happened to effect so striking a change? Ah! Away to the right we can make out through the haze the rude, ungainly timbers of the Pile Light. It is not much to look at; but it is at least a fixture. It is something to argue from. A shag stands perched upon it, craning his neck and staring timidly at us. Perhaps the strange appearance of the enshrouded ship alarms him, for, when we get abreast of him, he spreads his wings and, keeping close to the surface of the water, flies to a more distant perch. Going at this rate we soon penetrate the bank of fog. The land breaks suddenly upon us. We are out in the sunshine again. The low, leaden wall of mist lies gloomily across the bay behind us. Before us are wharves, houses, trees, the entrance to the river, and the city in the distance. The sighting of the Pile Light made just all the difference.

It always does. He is the skilful mariner whose vigilant and practised eye is swift to discern, amidst the haze of shifting things, life's fixed and stable qualities. The captain on the bridge saw the Pile Light long before I did. I felt the new and confident movement of the ship, and looked about in surprise for an explanation of the change. The sighting of the Pile Light marked the transition from doubt to certainty. And life knows no greater transition than that. Those who have followed the adventures of George Fielding in *It is Never Too Late to Mend* will remember the search for the lost cattle. George took Jacky, the black fellow, and they set out under a broiling Australian sun. Presently Jacky broke the silence abruptly.

'I find one,' said he.

'Where? Where?' cried George, looking all round. Jacky pointed to a rising ground at least six miles off.

George groaned. 'Are you making a fool of me? I can see nothing but a barren hill with a few great bushes here and there. You are never taking those bushes for beasts?'

Jacky smiled with utter scorn. 'White fellow stupid fellow; he see nothing.'

'Well, and what does black fellow see?' snapped George.

'Black fellow see a crow coming from the sun, and when he came over there he turned and went down and not get up again a good while. Then black fellow say, "*I think!*" Presently come flying one more crow from that other side where the sun is not. Black fellow watch him, and when he come over there he turn round and go down too, and not get up a good while. Then black fellow say, "*I know!*"'

They tramped the six miles, climbed the hill, and found one of George's best bullocks at its last gasp, with tongue protruding, a crow perched upon its ribs.

'*I think!*' said Jacky to himself; and in his uncertainty he simply sauntered by his puzzled master's side, and kept his eyes wide open.

'*I know!*' said Jacky; and with that brave confession came his master's enlightenment and a new and brisker pace.

'*I think!*' said the captain of the Loongana; and we crawled slowly and painfully and cautiously forward.

'*I know!*' said the captain of the Loongana on sighting the Pile Light; and the whole behaviour of the ship was changed.

Life holds few greater transitions than that notable transition from the realm of '*I think!*' to the realm of '*I know!*' Carlyle never forgot the hour of that transition. 'It is from that hour,' he says, 'that I date my spiritual new birth, or Baphometic Fire-Baptism; perhaps I directly thereupon began to be a man!' 'What was it,' asks Dr. Fitchett, in his *Life of Wesley*, 'what was it that happened in that little room in Aldersgate Street on the night of May 24, 1738? Something did happen; something memorable; something enduring. It changed Wesley's life. It transfigured weakness into power. Nay, it did something more: it changed the course of history.' And what was it? It was, Dr. Fitchett says, the passage of Wesley's soul from the realm of doubt to the realm of certainty. That night Wesley sighted the Pile Light; caught a glimpse of things that are immovable; and his life took on a new spirit and a new temper in consequence.

A very similar experience visited the soul of John Bunyan. 'After I had been in this miserable condition some three or four days, as I was sitting by the fire, I suddenly felt this word to sound in my heart, "*I must go to Jesus.*" At this my former darkness and atheism fled away, and the blessed things of heaven were set in my view. While I was on this sudden thus overtaken with surprise, "Wife," said I, "now I know! *I know!*" Oh, that night was a good night to me. I never knew but few better. I longed for the company of some of God's people, that I might have imparted to them what God had showed me. Christ was a precious Christ to my soul that night. I could scarce lie in bed for joy and peace and triumph through Christ!' Bunyan had sighted the Pile Light.

It is wonderful how little we need to see. The captain on the bridge could not see the land, nor the houses, nor the trees, nor any of the thousand and one things that he could generally see from that spot. But he could see *one* fixed object, and that sufficed him. I used to think that, before my soul could move forward with confidence, she must see everything. I thought that, before I could venture with any assurance upon the religious life, I must understand the story of Creation, must grasp the wonder of the miracles, must have some theory of the Atonement, must understand the Inspiration of the Scriptures, and must be able to prove the immortality of the soul. I fancied that it was necessary, before proceeding with confidence, to see the trees and the houses and the towers of the distant city. 'Unless all these are clear to me,' I said to myself, 'I can never make the port!' I have since discovered my mistake. I do not need to see the houses and the trees and the things along the shore; I only need to see the Pile Light. I do not need to see *everything*; I only need to see *something*.

I have a life with Christ to live,
But, ere I live it, must I wait
Till learning can clear answer give
Of this and that book's date?
I have a life in Christ to live,
I have a death in Christ to die;
And must I wait till Science give
All doubts a full reply?

Nay, rather, while the sea of doubt
Is raging wildly round about.
Questioning of life and death and sin,
Let me but creep within
Thy fold, O Christ, and at Thy feet
Take but the lowest seat.
And hear Thine awful voice repeat
In gentlest accents, heavenly sweet,
'Come unto Me and rest;
Believe Me and be blest!'

That is all; but it is enough. It is not everything; but it is the Pile Light standing out bravely through the mist. As soon as we saw the Pile Light, we quickly left the fog behind us. So did Bunyan. 'Wife,' said he, 'I must go to Jesus!' And 'at this my former darkness and atheism fled away, and the blessed things of heaven were set in my view.' That is the precise counterpart of our experience in the Bay.

'What are your speculations?' asked a friend who stood beside the death-bed of Michael Faraday.

'Speculations?' he replied in astonishment. 'Speculations? I have none. I know whom I have believed. I rest my soul upon certainties!'

It is a great thing, when the mists of death are closing in on every side, to approach the last report with the outline of the Pile Light in full view!

IV - Marjorie

Marjorie is ninety-two, although you would never suspect it. Her hair is as black as it was when, more than seventy years ago, her tall young lover first stroked it. Marjorie is English — as English as English can be. The fact stares you in the face as soon as you put your hand to the latch of her gate. For the little front garden is the condensed essence of England. It is as English as the garden of a Kentish cottage. You inhale the scent-laden English air as you walk down the path to Marjorie's door. You drink in the fragrance of the roses and the wallflowers, the sweet-peas and the jasmine, the carnations and the gillyflowers, the musk and mignonette; and then, as you pause for a moment in the porch, awaiting the opening of the door, the soft petals of the honeysuckle brush against your face. They must all be flowers of rich perfume to be of any use to Marjorie now, for Marjorie is blind. I had been in conversation with her for some time before I realized that the eyes that seemed to look so wistfully into mine were unable to convey any impression to her alert and hungry mind. Her sightless eyes and the slight stoop at the shoulders are the only indications that she gives you of her heavy burden of years. She cannot see the pictures on the wall, representing the scenes of her childhood — the village street with its comfortable inn and its odd medley of stores; the thickly wooded lane in which she so often found nuts and blackberries; the fields of golden buttercups; and the village green with its rustic seats and shady grove of oaks. She cannot see these pictures now; but she says that the scenes all come back to her, as clearly as if she had visited them yesterday, when she sits out in the porch, luxuriating in the fragrance of the flowers, listening to the droning of the bees, and enjoying the song of the thrush who sings to her from his perch in the lilac by the side of the house.

Even if I, like Marjorie, live to be ninety-two, I shall never forget that first visit that I paid her. It came about very simply. 'I wish,' said a gentleman, as he left the service on Sunday morning, 'I wish you could find time to call on my old mother. She *would* appreciate it.' He gave me the address, and I set out the very next day, little dreaming that so very ordinary a mission was destined to bring into my life so wealthy an enrichment. Very abruptly sometimes life's casual ministries unlock for us the gates of gold. We turn a bend in a dusty road, and catch a glimpse of Paradise. We reach unexpectedly the brow of a hill, and obtain a vision of infinity. So was it with me that day.

As I sat in the cosy little parlour awaiting the old lady's entrance, I expected that I should have to make the conversation, and I wondered how I could best secure that it should serve some profitable end. I smile now at the ignorance that led me into such a line of cogitation. I had not then met Marjorie. When she entered the room, the conversation made itself. I had simply nothing to do with it. I came to minister; but I found myself being ministered to.

Not for a moment do I suggest that Marjorie was what Bunyan would call a brisk talker on matters of religion. She was far too reverent and far too modest for that. I mean rather that she had something really great to say, and she said it really greatly. Hers was the grand style, glorified by transparent sincerity. Her speech was dignified and stately, whilst her voice was tremulous with deep emotion. There was a majesty about her very diction. She employed phrases that are never now heard, and that are only to be found in the mellow pages of a school book never now read. Outside a second-hand bookshop you may often see a box into which the desperate dealer has thrown all his rubbish, offering it to an unappreciative public at a nominal price of a penny a volume. To turn over this ill-assorted collection of literary flotsam and jetsam is as interesting and pathetic as to wander through the casual ward of a workhouse. No two cases are alike, yet all have come to this!

Here in the box is a Spanish grammar, badly torn; there, too, is the second part of a three-volume novel. Like Euclid's ideal circle, it is without beginning and without ending. Yonder is the guide-book to a long-forgotten exhibition. Such a higgledy-piggledy box! But if you delve a little more deeply, you will be sure to come upon some old volumes of eighteenth-century sermons. The leather backs are badly broken, and the leaves are yellow with age. But if you will sacrifice the necessary penny and go to the trouble of carrying one of these old volumes home, you will find the very vocabulary to which I listened as I sat that day in Marjorie's pretty little parlour. Yet, as this dead language fell from Marjorie's lips, it came to life again! It was full of energy and vigour; it was instinct with spiritual significance and with holy passion. It throbbed and quivered and glowed and flashed. It was as if some ancestral castle that had stood deserted and gloomy for a century had been suddenly inhabited, and was now ablaze with light and vibrant with shouts and laughter. The antique phrases simply sparkled with vitality as they tripped from her tongue. It was, as I say, a great story greatly told. Marjorie had been buffeted in a long, stern struggle; she had known heart-break and agony and tears; yet her memory remained at ninety-two absolutely unclouded, and her lip retained its power of forceful utterance. And sitting there in her cosy parlour, whilst the breath of the garden came pouring in through the open window, did Marjorie unfold to me the treasures of her rich experience.

'Ah, yes,' she replied, with a smile, when I made some reference to the remarkable length of her pilgrimage, 'I was only a girl when I entered into the sweetness of religion.' The phrase, illumined by that bright though sightless smile, and interpreted by accents so full of feeling, fastened upon my memory at once. *'The sweetness of religion.'* 'I was only a girl when I entered into *the sweetness of religion!'* And then she went on to tell me of the rapture of her first faith. Seventy-five years earlier, religion had come into her life like a great burst of song. Amidst the sunshine of an English summertime, whilst the fields were redolent of clover and of new-mown hay, her girlish soul had sought and found the Saviour. Instantly the whole world had stood transfigured. Her tongue seemed to catch fire as she told me of the radiant experiences of those never-to-be-forgotten days. I saw, as I listened, that the soul has a rhetoric of its own, an eloquence with which no acquired oratory can compare. She told of the joy that she found in her own secret communion with the Lord, sometimes in the quietude of her little room — the room with the projecting lattice window from which she loved to watch the mists rising from the hollow as the sun came up over the hills; sometimes down among the alders along the banks of the stream, sitting so still that the rabbits would scurry up and down the green banks without taking the slightest notice of her; sometimes in long, delicious rambles across the open park — rambles in which she was only disturbed by the swish of a frightened pheasant or the tramp of fallow deer; and sometimes amidst the leafy seclusion of the primrosed woods. And often, at sunset, when Dapple and Brownie had been milked, and the tea-things put away, she would take her knitting and saunter down the dusty old road. And as, one by one, the stars peeped out, and the nightingale called from the woods in the valley, and glowworms shone in the grass under the hedge, and a bat flapped and fluttered in its queer flight round her head, it seemed as though the miracle of Emmaus were repeated, and Jesus came and walked with her. She spoke of the wonders that, under such conditions, broke upon her spirit like a light from heaven. Her Bible became a new book to her; and an unspeakable glory fell upon the village sanctuary, the dearest spot on earth to her in those days of long ago. A wave of happy recollection swept over her as she told of the walks along the lanes and across the fields, in the company of a group of kindred spirits, to attend those simple but memorable services. The path led through a tossing sea of harebells and cowslips; the lane was redolent of hawthorn and sweet-brier. As they made their way to the church that peeped shyly through the foliage of the clump of elms on the hill, the solemn monotone of its insistent bell mingled with the chatter of the finches in the hedges and the blither note of the lark high up in the blue. Marjorie's blind eyes almost shone as she recalled, and, with glowing tongue, recounted, all these precious and beautiful memories. 'I was only a girl,' she said, 'when I entered into the sweetness of religion!'

'But,' I interjected, 'you speak of the sweetness of religion as though it were a thing of long ago. Do you mean that it became exhausted? Did that happy phase of your Christian experience fade away?'

A cloud passed over her face like the shadow that, on a summer's afternoon, will sometimes float over the corn.

'Oh, well, you know,' she replied, after a thoughtful pause, 'the tone of one's life changes with the years. I left my girlhood behind me. I married; children came to our home in quick succession; life became a battle rather than a frolic; and sometimes the struggle was almost grim. Then troubles fell thick and fast upon me. In one dreadful week I buried two of my boys, one on the Tuesday and the other on the Friday. Then, last of all, my husband, the soul of my soul, the best man I have ever known, was snatched rudely from my side.'

Marjorie hid her face for a moment in her hands. At last my impatience compelled me to break the silence.

'And do you mean,' I inquired, 'do you mean that, under the stress of all this sorrow, you lost *the sweetness of religion?*'

'Well,' she replied thoughtfully, 'under such conditions you would scarcely speak of *sweetness.* I would rather say that, during those sterner years, I entered into *the power of religion.*'

A ring, almost of triumph, came into her voice.

'Yes,' she said, 'in those years I entered into *the power of religion.* Only once did my faith really stagger. It was on the night of that second funeral — that second funeral within a single week! I was kneeling in my own room on the spot on which I had knelt, morning and evening, through all the years. But I could not pray. I felt that God had failed and forsaken me. My shrine was empty, and I burst into tears. And then, all at once, a Hand seemed laid gently upon my shoulder and a Voice sounded in my ear. "Am I a man that I should lie?" it said. I was startled. I felt chastened and rebuked. I had treated Him as though He were no wiser than I, and as though He had broken His word. Then, through my tears, I prayed as I had never been able to pray before. A great peace soothed my broken spirit. I was ashamed of my distrust. It was the only time my faith had wavered. No; I should not speak of *sweetness* as I recall those years of bitter sorrow and sore struggle. In those days I entered into *the power of religion!'*

'But now look, Marjorie,' I pleaded, 'you tell me that, as a girl, you entered into *the sweetness of religion,* and that, in the graver years that followed, you entered into the *power of religion.* But your girlhood and your struggle have both passed now, and here you are in this quiet little cottage looking back across the intervening years at those far-away periods. Would you say that you now enjoy the *sweetness* or the *power?'*

Her face shone; it was almost seraphic. Her whole being became suddenly animated and luminous. She reached out her hands towards me as though she held something in each of them.

'I have them both!' she cried in a perfect transport of delight. *'I have them both!* The *sweetness* that I knew in my English girlhood has come back to me in the days of my old age; and the *power* that came to me in the years of trial and loss has never since forsaken me. I have them both; oh, bless His holy Name, *I have them both!'*

It was too much for her. Overcome by the rush of recollection and the tempest of exultant emotion, she sank back in her chair and lapsed into silence.

'Why, Marjorie,' I said, 'you have given me the very thing I wanted. As I walked along the road I was wondering what I should preach about on Sunday. But I know now. I shall preach on those words from the swan-song of Moses in which the old leader, in laying down his charge, bears grateful witness to God's goodness to Israel. "He made him," he says, "to suck *honey out of the rock."* I was reading in a book of travel only yesterday that in the Orient the wild bees store their honey in the crevices among the cliffs, and on a hot day you may see it trickling down the face of the granite in shining streams of sweetness! As a girl, you say, you entered into *the sweetness of religion.* As a girl, girl-like, you gave little thought to the rock itself, but you loved to taste the sweetness of the honey. You entered into *the sweetness of religion!* But, as a woman, in the turmoil and tussle of life, buffeted and storm-beaten, you forgot the honey that oozed from the cracks and fissures, and were glad to feel the massive strength of the rock itself beneath your feet. You entered into *the power of religion!* And now, the fury of the storm all overpast, you tell me that you still rest upon the great rock, rejoicing in its firmness; and, as in your earlier days, you once more enjoy the honey that exudes from its recesses. You enjoy both the strength and the sweetness; *you have them both!* "With honey out of the rock have I satisfied thee!" I shall certainly preach on that text on Sunday!' And I did.

V - Camouflage

New occasions teach new duties — and new dictions. The War has given us a new word, and a very interesting one. 'Camouflage' has become a commonplace. In its original French setting it simply means to be concealed in smoke. I fancy I detect in it a hint that very noisome things may be made to serve very noble ends. The big battleships certainly thought so. When harassed by the fatal but elusive submarines, the huge Dreadnoughts hid themselves behind thick screens of impenetrable smoke, and were saved by camouflage. Having once been applied to tactics of the kind, the vivid expression was soon used to connote a multitude of similar manoeuvres. Guns cunningly concealed amidst waving forestry; men smothered with wisps of hay or fronds of fern or twigs of trees; ships painted with fantastic designs, calculated to conceal their true identity, — all this has come to be known as camouflage. Ian Hay quotes Major Wagstaffe as saying that 'you can now disguise anything as anything. For instance, you can make up a battery of six-inch guns to look like a flock of sheep, and herd them into action browsing. Or you can dispatch a scouting party across No Man's Land dressed up as pillar-boxes, so that a deluded enemy, instead of opening fire with a machine-gun, will merely post letters in them — valuable letters, containing military secrets!' This, surely, is the perfection of camouflage!

If, however, the word is new to us, the thing itself is as old as the hills. Has not Sir Walter Scott told us how, at Flodden, the Scottish army set fire to its tents and charged the English host under cover of the smoke? Moreover, camouflage is the watchword of the wilds. In his *Tropical Africa* Henry Drummond does not use the word, but he has a chapter about it all the same. Nature, he says, is one vast system of imposture. 'Carlyle in his blackest visions of shams and humbugs among humankind never saw anything so finished in hypocrisy as the naturalist finds in every tropical forest. There are to be seen creatures, not singly, but in tens of thousands, whose very appearance, down to the minutest spot and wrinkle, is an affront to truth, whose every attitude is a pose for a purpose, and whose whole life is a sustained lie. Before these masterpieces of deception the most ingenious of human impositions are vulgar and transparent. Fraud is not only the great rule of life in a tropical forest, but the one condition of it.' And then he proceeds to give examples. One day he found a bit of dried grass lying on his shoulder. The natives cried out in alarm and pointed to it. Drummond could not understand their excitement. He picked up the grass and examined it. They cried out that it was 'chirombo' — it was alive! He was incredulous, but they soon proved to him that their statement was true. It was an insect practising camouflage. Half a dozen pages farther on the Professor gives a photograph of a leaf-insect. To look at the picture, you could declare that it was a leaf, pure and simple. The shape is the shape of a leaf; there is the stem, sturdy at the base and tapering away towards the point; there are the fibres running out from the main stem towards the rough edges; in every minutest particular the thing is a precise replica of the leaves round about it. But, again, it is an insect — an insect practising camouflage! And then the narrative takes an almost tragic turn. One of the most beautiful and ornate of all the tropical reptiles, and one of the most deadly, is the puff-adder. 'It is essentially a forest animal, its true habitat being among the fallen leaves in the deep shade of the trees by the banks of streams. Now, in such a position, at the distance of a foot or two, its appearance so exactly resembles the forest bed as to be almost indistinguishable from it. I was once just throwing myself down under a tree to rest when, stooping to clear the spot, I noticed a peculiar pattern among the leaves. I started back in horror to find a puff-adder of the largest size, its thick back only visible, and its fangs within a few inches of my face as I stooped. It was lying concealed among fallen leaves so like itself that, but for the exceptional caution which in African travel becomes a habit, I should certainly have sat down upon it, and to sit down upon a puffadder is to sit down for the last time.' The loathsome brute was practising a camouflage which almost deprived the world of one of the most gracious and inspiring ministries of the nineteenth century.

But we need not have gone to Central Africa. Camouflage is everywhere. I find it in my Bible. David resorted to camouflage on a very famous occasion. He was a monarch, and he tried to pass himself off as a maniac! 'He feigned himself mad in their hands, and scrabbled on the doors of the gate, and let his spittle fall down upon his beard.' David Livingstone's great-grandfather, Gavin Hunter, was once thrown into Hamilton Jail for a technical offence which, in point of fact, was rather to his credit than otherwise. But just at that time all prisoners were being shipped off to the wars or to the plantations. Poor Gavin was in great trouble. He thought of his wife and his three little children, who would starve if he were sent overseas. In his distress he turned to his Bible, and chanced to light upon this very passage concerning David. He resolved to adopt a similar ruse. When the sergeant visited his cell, he was astounded. Then, pitying poor Gavin, he interrupted his ravings by asking a question. 'Tell me, gudeman,' he said, 'are you really out of your mind? I'll befriend you.' Gavin detected a note of sympathy in his voice, and told the whole story. The sergeant reported the affair to the officer in charge of the jail, who visited Gavin in person. 'Tak' that, gudeman,' he said, giving him some silver, 'and gang awa' hame to your wife and your weans!' David Livingstone's mother told her distinguished son this story of successful camouflage on her death-bed, in the course of the explorer's visit to Scotland in 1864. 'Ay,' she said, smiling, 'and mony a prayer went up from our hame for that sergeant, for my grandfather was an unco godly man. He never had so much money in his life before!' A curious story this of deliverance and enrichment by way of camouflage.

I confess to a little surprise that Professor Drummond should charge the leaf-insect, the puff-adder, and all the other artists of the wild with hypocrisy. Are they really hypocritical? We must distinguish between things that differ;

and there is all the difference In the world between camouflage and hypocrisy. Hypocrisy is the attempt of a mean thing to pass Itself off as a mighty thing; camouflage is the attempt of a mighty thing to pass Itself off as a mean thing. If a cloud of smoke tries to pass itself off as a battleship, that Is hypocrisy; but If a battleship tries to pass Itself off as a cloud of smoke, that Is camouflage! If a fallen tree tries to pass itself off as a big gun, that Is hypocrisy; but If a big gun tries to pass itself off as a fallen tree, that Is camouflage!

Aesop has a fable entitled 'The Ass in the Lion's Skin.' Now an ass in a lion's skin is not practising camouflage; he is playing the hypocrite, that is all. But if, on the other hand, a lion were to don the skin of an ass, he would be resorting to camouflage! If a scarecrow ever scared a crow — and there is no record of such a wild improbability — he scared him by his downright hypocrisy. But if, in order to watch a house in which a burglary is expected, a detective posts himself in the garden in the guise of a scarecrow, that detective is practising the arts of camouflage! There is clearly an essential difference between an old broom and a suit of clothes masquerading as a man, and a man pretending to be only an old broom and a suit of clothes. The one is a humbug; the other is a tactician.

The most pathetic instance known to me of the use of camouflage occurs in Ian Maclaren's *Drumsheugh's Love Story.* All the Glen knew Drumsheugh as the man of the close fist, mean, hard, niggardly. He drove every bargain to the uttermost farthing. At last he grew to be old; he was nearly eighty. He looked round and discovered that all the comrades of his early days, and all the friends of his lustier years, had dropped into their graves — all but one. That one was William Maclure, the doctor of Drumtochty. And then a strange desire awoke the soul of Drumsheugh. He felt that, before he too went the way of all flesh, he should like to open his heart to the doctor, and tell him the secret that had been buried in his breast for years. One cruel winter's day the doctor, almost frozen, came riding on Jess, his brave little pony, up the Glen, fighting his way through the deep snow-drifts. Drumsheugh called him in, sat him by the fireside and entertained him royally. Then the two old men sat looking into the dying embers, seeing visions of the days of auld lang syne. The hour had come. Drumsheugh unlocked his lips, and told his tale.

As a youth he had loved Marget, the sweetest girl in all the Glen. He had counted it heaven to look into her winsome face, to listen to her soft rich voice, to watch her gentle ways. Once, in a cornfield, her soft hand had touched his, and the thrill of that exquisite moment had been with him all down the years. Once she dropped a flower, and he had treasured it, even to grey hairs. But he had never found the courage to declare his love; and one summer evening she met him by chance, at a stile across the fields, and told him that she was going to be married! Poor Drumsheugh clung to the stile, dazed, for hours, like a man suddenly bereft of everything.

Marget married, and everything went ill with her. And then Drumsheugh made his brave resolve. He scraped and pinched and saved; and sent every penny to her through a firm of solicitors, who were instructed to say that it came from a relative in America. But for this, Marget would have been turned out of house and home; she could never have paid the doctor's bills; she could never have sent her boy to college.

'Drumsheugh,' cried the doctor at last, 'Drumsheugh, ye're the maist accomplished leer 'at's ever been born in Drumtochty, an'…th' best man a' ever saw!'

Now here is the question. Was Drumsheugh a hypocrite? How could he be a hypocrite, and yet be the best man that the old doctor had ever seen? He was an expert in camouflage, that was all!

But it was a mistake. Drumsheugh came to feel that it was a mistake. Marget, an old, old woman now, discovered the deception at last. She came to Drumsheugh and blessed him through her tears.

'He took her hand, and made as though he would have raised it to his lips, but, as he bent, she kissed him on the forehead. "This," she said, "for yir great and faithfu' love!"'

Yes, it was a mistake. Drumsheugh felt that he would have been happier and better if he had contrived to maintain his noble and unselfish ministry to Marget without gaining for himself so odious a reputation in the Glen. It was a poignant anguish to him that all his old schoolfellows and companions had gone down to their graves despising him.

His camouflage was a mistake. Camouflage is often a mistake. I shall never forget the night on which I said farewell to Mosgiel. The manse — our home through twelve long, happy years — was dismantled; the rooms were almost empty; the walls and floors were bare. The farewell-meeting was held. It was late when I reached home to sleep for the last time under the old roof. Just as I was turning into the gate a figure emerged from the hedge. It was a woman; a young woman who, through all my ministry, had regularly attended the services of the church. She was weeping bitterly. I led her into the empty manse; she sat upon one packing-case, and I upon another.

'Oh, I've been wicked, wicked, wicked!' she cried. 'I've come to church, and gone out again, and I've always pretended that I did not care. And when you spoke to me, I told you that I did not wish to be a Christian or to take any step towards a holier life. And all the while my heart has been aching — almost breaking. When Communion nights came, and I saw other women remain to partake of it, I felt that I would give the light of my eyes to be able to sit at the Table with them; but I went out into the dark and laughed it off. And when, on other occasions, I saw other women helping in the work, I felt that I would give all I possessed to be helping too. But I went through with it, and always said I did not care.' It was a great piece of camouflage; and bitterly did she repent it. We kneeled together on the bare boards, and whilst I prayed, her heart uttered itself in sobs of deep contrition. And so I said farewell to my old home and my old church, and she said farewell to her long, long camouflage! I like to think of that closing episode of my first ministry; and I delight in knowing that, whilst I have been labouring on other shores, she has remained among the most devoted and consistent members of the Mosgiel church.

VI - The Whaler

Whales are great sport. We have all done a little whaling in our time. I shall never forget the months that I spent amongst lances, harpoons, reels, lines, and blubber. There is no accounting for the vagaries of the law of association; and oddly enough, I cannot even think about whales without harking back to a certain lofty haystack that stood not very far from my old English home. I remember, as vividly as though it were but yesterday, that I had spent a good part of one memorable winter curled up in my father's spacious arm-chair, reading all that R. M. Ballantyne, Mayne Reid, and Fenimore Cooper could tell me about Red Indians and grizzly bears. Now Red Indians and grizzly bears are first-rate, as every schoolboy knows; but you can have too much even of a good thing; and, by the time that the fields were once more golden with buttercups, my familiarity with the furry wigwams and the Rocky Mountains had engendered an inevitable contempt. I had seen enough of the scalps of the braves and the skins of the bears to last me for many a long day; and it was at this critical juncture that a whaling story fell into my hands. It swept me off my feet, took my soul by storm, captivated my whole imagination. I begged, borrowed, or bought all the tales of whaling adventure that were anywhere procurable. And whenever, in the perusal of those thrilling pages, I heard from the crow's-nest the rousing cry of 'There she spouts!' I crept stealthily off to the haystack, and, sprawling at full length, enjoyed, without interruption, the terrific excitements of the chase. My prone body sank of its own weight into the soft and odorous hay, rendering me quite invisible; and in this safe retreat I was dead to all the world, and all the world was dead to me. How many times on that old haystack I watched the huge monster describe his vast circles round the ship! How many times I held my breath as he suddenly appeared, a tense mass of quivering rage, within a few yards of the boat! How many times I saw the glittering harpoon bury itself in his soft hot flesh, and heard the shriek of the rushing line as it flew from the whirring wheel! How many times I found myself swimming for dear life after the infuriated creature had smashed our little boat to splinters! How often, too, I felt my cheeks flush with the fierce joy of capture, and could scarcely believe my eyes when I looked round and discovered that, instead of being on the oily deck of a whaler, I was lying full length on the top of a haystack!

II

But how am I to account for this strange gust of recollection? It was my Bible that started it. At the opening of Job's penultimate chapter I came abruptly on a question that first made me smile, and then made me think — *'Canst thou catch a whale with a fish-hook?'* If I, as an old whaler, understand the position rightly, it is designed, by this grotesque interrogation, to expose some very common fallacies. There is, for example, the folly of supposing that a whale can be caught with a fish-hook. Every whaler knows quite well that it is ludicrously impossible. As an old whaler I can bear witness to the fact that the experience of life has taught me that there must be a certain proportion between the end that you hope to compass and the means that you employ in order to attain it. I have caught a minnow with a bent pin and a yard of string; but I have never been able to land a salmon with that gear. In Job the argument is pushed yet another step. To him the capture of a whale seemed a sheer impossibility. The ancients saw the huge beast disporting himself in the blue waters; but in their wildest imaginings they never dreamed that a day would come in which men would seek to make him their prey. And, indeed, it was not until about a thousand years ago that some hardy Norseman, of tough sinews and still tougher soul, conceived the idea of scouring the seas in pursuit of such big game. Job may have listened in awe to tales that sailors told concerning the frightful monsters they had seen upon the deep, and, if so, he was prepared for the question — *'Canst thou catch a whale with a fishhook?'* You can catch a minnow with a bent pin; but not a salmon! You can catch a salmon with a hook; but not a whale!

Old Peggy Dodson runs a flower-stall. For many a long year she has stood, summer and winter, at the corner of Princes and Edgecumbe streets, just against Barnards' great drapery store. Her violets and jonquils are said to be the best that can be got, and many of the great ladies who come in and out of Barnards' slip a big bunch of them into their motors before setting out for home. Peggy only aims at making a couple of pounds a week just to keep body and soul together, and she contrives to do it by the investment of a very modest capital. But Barnards' would not be content with a profit of a couple of pounds a week. Mr. Edward Barnard lives in a palatial residence out at Brockville Park. To keep things going he needs a profit a hundred times as large as Peggy's. And because he wishes to draw a hundred times as much out of his business, he puts a hundred times as much into his business. The sum that he pays out every week in rent, wages, and stock is amazing! But he signs those cheques with a light heart because he knows that, by a law that is as fixed as the law of gravitation, there must be a certain proportion between the end that you desire to compass and the means that you employ to attain it. You can't earn Barnards' profits by the investment of Peggy's capital. You can't catch whales with fish-hooks!

Many years ago I knew two sisters who were both Sunday-school teachers. Sheila was a lively girl, and everybody was very fond of her; but she rarely took things seriously. On Sunday, as soon as dinner was over, she got her Bible and her *Teacher's Helps,* to see what the lesson was all about. And then, marking a few passages that she thought might be read aloud to the scholars, she dotted down a few notes before scampering off to school. Sometimes, when dinner was late, or the conversation at table particularly interesting and protracted, she was compelled to study the lesson as she hurried down the streets, sometimes in company. Mary, on the other hand, regarded her class as part of life's great adventure. She allowed the coming Sunday's lesson to simmer in her mind all through the week, and found untold delight in wrestling with the various problems it presented. She was a welcome guest in the homes of all her boys; and if one of them failed to appear on the Sunday afternoon, Mary was like a hen with a missing chick. She even wove those roguish faces into her prayers, and, indeed, found it easier to admit them than to exclude them. Anybody who knew the two sisters as intimately as I did could see that Sheila was like Old Peggy, whilst Mary was like Mr. Barnard. Sheila put very little into her class, and drew very little out; Mary lavished all her thought and devotion upon it, and found in it the delight of her life. I have met many of those boys, now full-grown men, during the past twenty years. It is with difficulty that you can recall Sheila to the remembrance of those who once sat at her feet; she flitted into their lives and flitted out again without leaving any permanent impression at all. But Mary's boys brighten at the very mention of her name. 'Whenever I have been tempted to do a mean thing or neglect a duty,' one of them said to me not long ago, 'I have thought of her; and the memory of her face has settled it!' And he spoke for them all. Sheila was angling with a piece of string and a bent pin; Mary was catching whales!

A mere novice in the art of living must have noticed that only the cheap prizes are cheaply won; the really precious things of life come to us through blood and agony and tears. And is not the kingdom of heaven to be numbered among those exceedingly precious things? Is it likely, therefore, that the kingdom of heaven can be cheaply gained?

'Just put up your hand; now, while every head is bowed; put up your hand, and the great transaction's done!'

I was passing the Miller's Point Mission-hall. A stirring chorus led me to pause, and, after the singing, these words fell upon my ear. It is not for me to judge. I had not listened to the address that had preceded this appeal. But, taken by themselves, the words seemed to me to imply that the salvation of the soul can be very cheaply secured. When I reached home I took down my *Pilgrim's Progress,* and reviewed afresh Christian's sustained and perilous exploit. And then I turned to the New Testament. The transition from the evangelist's appeal to these noble volumes on my table was like the transition from the angler's dangling line to the stern and hazardous struggle of the whaler. For my New Testament warns me on every page that whales are not to be caught with fish-hooks. Gold does not lie about the street-corners. The kingdom of heaven suffereth violence, and the violent take it by storm. I am to strive, to wrestle, to agonize, in my resolute and persistent endeavour to enter in at the strait gate. Only through much tribulation, so I am told, can I hope to enter the Kingdom. The New Testament writers were whalers, not anglers. Their phraseology is the phraseology of the fierce and desperate conflict; it throbs with vehemence and intensity; it is suggestive of long and anxious and sustained adventure. And who can help noticing that when it tells of one who set His face, like a flint, to win the greatest prize of all, it makes it clear that He only attained His end, and finished His work, and gained His crown after a struggle unparalleled in the annals of human enterprise and achievement?

III

It is foolish to match the mean against the mighty. The contrast between the whale on the one hand and the angler's puny little line on the other is intended to provoke a smile. I should have loved to have seen old Izaak Walton's face when, in the course of his riverside devotions, he lit upon this passage! How could Job angle for a whale? As the following verses point out, 'he has no bait wherewith to deceive him, no hook wherewith to catch him, no line wherewith to draw him out of the water, no reed to run through his gills, and no thorn on which to carry him home.' The whole conception is extraordinary, whimsical, grotesque. It is the wave fighting against the cliff, the mouse fighting against the lion, the pigmy fighting against the giant. What does it all mean?

If good old Izaak Walton, resting under the alders on the green banks of the Itchen or the Dove, examined the context in order to ascertain the meaning of the curious inquiry, he must have found himself suddenly and startlingly transported from the realm of the ludicrous to the realm of the sublime. For see! 'Then answered the Lord unto Job out of the whirlwind, and said. *Canst thou catch a whale with a fish-hook?* or his tongue with a line that thou lettest down? None is so fierce that dare stir him up: *who then is able to stand against Me?*' Here is a swift transition from comedy to tragedy! At the beginning of the drama Job loses his asses, his oxen, his camels, his children, and his health. In the course of the years Job is tempted to murmur against God, and to impeach the justice of the Most High. And this is the answer that comes to him out of the whirlwind — 'Canst thou catch a whale with a fish-hook? How then cartst thou stand against Me?' And Job humbles himself, and kisses the hand that he had spurned, and the great drama closes amidst the tears and smiles of reconciliation.

At the opening and at the close of the inspired records I find two brave, heroic figures. In one respect these two — Job and Paul — are very much alike. The culminating point in the experience of Job was his discovery that his rebellion against the Divine Will was as futile and as foolish as the fishing-line with which an angler might endeavour to compass the destruction of a whale. The culminating point in the experience of Paul was his discovery that his persecution of the infant Church was a raid upon Omnipotence. 'And he fell to the earth, and heard a voice saying unto him, Saul, Saul, why persecutest thou Me? And he said. Who art Thou, Lord? And the Lord said, I am Jesus whom thou persecutest; it is hard for thee to kick against the pricks!'

And, like Job, Paul abandoned the unequal contest, and kissed the hand that he had sought to crucify.

'How canst thou stand against *Me?*' said the voice to Job.

'Why persecutest thou *Me?*' said the voice to Paul.

And Job and Paul both discovered that the day on which a man submits his stubborn heart to the will of heaven is the day on which all heaven comes pouring into that penitent and contrite heart.

VII - A Box of Perfume

The smell of things! The smell of things! What a box of perfume this old world of ours is, to be sure! I was reading only yesterday Mr. E. V. Lucas's Essay on Rupert Brooke. Mr. Lucas turns aside to chat entertainingly about his own tastes and fancies. 'I find,' he says, 'that, on my list of loves, scents would take a very important place — the scent of gorse blossoms rubbed in the hand and then crushed against the face, the scent of geranium leaves or the leaves of the lemon verbena, the scent of pine-trees, the scent of unlit cigars, the scent of cigarette smoke blown my way from a distance, the scent of coffee as it arrives from the grocer's, the scent of the underside of those little cushions of moss which come away so easily in the woods, the scent of lilies of the valley, the scent of oatcake for cattle, the scent of lilac, and, for reasons, above all, perhaps, the scent of a rubbish fire in the garden.' Richard Jefferies has a notable passage of which this forcibly reminded me. 'There ain't nothing,' he makes his old gamekeeper say, 'there ain't nothing to compare with the smell of the woods. You should just come out here in the spring and sniff up the scent of that there oak bark. It goes right down your throat, and preserves your lungs as the tan do leather. And I've heard say as folks who work in the tanyards never have no illness. There's always a smell from the trees, dead or living, and I could tell what wood a log was in the dark by my nose. The air is better where the woods be. There's the smell of the earth, too; 'specially just as the plough turns it up. It's a fine thing; and the hedges and the grass are as sweet as sugar after a shower.' But enough of this! I did not set out to catalogue the perfumes in the box; but to philosophize about them, and especially to ask myself the reason for their presence there.

For, only this afternoon, I was sitting with some friends upon the lawn — itself an odorous place — telling of the holiday tour from which I have just returned. In doing so, I was impressed by the way in which memory revived, and description became easy, whenever I chanced to mention the smell of things. The smell of the bush; the smell of the earth; the smell of the hay; the smell of the hops; the smell of the hedges; the smell of the gardens, — at every such reference the beauty of the landscape rushed back upon my mind in vivid detail; and the tongue set off afresh with its pleasant task of reminiscence.

I have noticed the same thing before. We have all noticed it. As Walter Savage Landor told us a hundred years ago,

> ...sweet scents,
> Are the swift vehicles of still sweeter thoughts,
> And nurse and pillow the dull memory
> That would let drop without them her best stores.
> They bring me tales of youth and tones of love.

Ah, to be sure, tales of youth! As a small boy I was sent to a private school for a year or two to prepare for the public school to which I went later. I do not know how long I remained there. I possess a history-book bearing my name and the date in the schoolmaster's handwriting. This proves that I was there at the age of seven; but as only the earlier pages are marked, I conclude that I must have left for the larger school shortly after. It was often a matter of regret to me that I could recall so little of my first school. The whole thing seemed to have departed from my mind. I remembered only the exterior of the building, the death of the schoolmaster, and a few very hazy impressions. But one day, more than twenty years afterwards, I was crossing a field and detected a peculiar odour. It arose from a plant upon which I had just trodden. Instantly the old school stood out before my mind as though I had only left it the day before. The porch, the schoolroom, the desk, the huge globes in the corner, the maps on the walls, the piano, the blackboard, and a hundred tiniest details rushed to mind one after the other, and have remained vividly there ever since. The plant on which I had just trodden grew on the green bank behind the school, and we boys used to press the leaves in our hands and inhale the fragrance that distilled from our scented fingers when poring over our lessons later on. I had never come across a plant of that species through all the years that intervened. I must have seen a thousand sights and heard a thousand sounds that should have opened the floodgates of memory; yet they had not the magic power. Their 'Open, Sesame!' was unheeded. But the spell lurked in the scent of the grass; and, thanks to it, my old school is now clearly photographed upon the tablets of my memory.

Here, then, is a singular thing: this connexion between a breath of perfume and a wave of memory! It does not, of course, always work out pleasantly. No law does. One is reminded of Dickens. In his early days he lived through a dismal and humiliating experience. He earned his living in a blacking factory. 'My work,' he says, 'was to cover the pots of blacking, first with a piece of oil-paper, and then with a piece of string; and then to clip the paper close and neat, all round, until it looked as smart as a pot of ointment from an apothecary's shop.' During that year or so — he himself has no notion how long it lasted — his misery was so intense that, to the end of his days, he never referred to it. He worked from early morning until late at night, and could only manage to live on his meagre salary by dividing it into six little parcels, marking each parcel with a day of the week, and steadfastly refusing to break into Saturday's parcel until Saturday came. When the hunger was unendurable, he used to take a turn at Covent Garden and stare at the pineapples, sniffing up as he did so the flavour of the faded cabbage leaves that everywhere littered the place. Close to the cellar in which he worked was a hat factory which emitted an odour peculiarly its own. In due course the boy was delivered from this abject and degrading phase of his existence. But the memory of it haunted him like a spectre. 'From that hour until this at which I write,' he says, in a letter written many years afterwards, 'from that hour until this no word of that part of my childhood has passed my lips. From that hour until this my father and my mother have been stricken dumb upon it. I have never heard the least allusion to it, however far off and remote, from either of them. I have never in any burst of confidence with any one, my own wife not excepted, raised the curtain I then dropped, thank God.' And he tells us that to the close of his life, whenever he caught the smell of decayed cabbage leaves, the smell of hat-making, or the smell of blacking, a shudder ran through his frame as he recalled his early miseries. 'I never had the courage,' he says, 'to go back to the place. I could not endure to go near it. For many years, when I came near to Robert Warren's, in the Strand, I crossed over to the opposite side of the way, to avoid a certain smell of the cement they put upon the blacking-corks which reminded me of what I once was.' The novelist's bitter experience is very suggestive. The *sight* of hats, blacking-bottles, or cabbage leaves seems to have had no effect upon him. But the *smell* of any of them almost paralysed him.

Beside this painful illustration relating to Charles Dickens, let me lay a pleasant illustration relating to George Gissing. 'I know men,' he makes Henry Ryecroft say, 'I know men who say they had as lief read any book in a library copy as in one from their own shelf. To me that is unintelligible. For one thing, I know every book of mine by its scent, and I have but to put my nose between the pages to be reminded of all sorts of things. My Gibbon, for instance, my well-bound eight-volume Milman edition, which I have read and read and read again for more than thirty years, never do I open it but the scent of the noble pages restores to me all the exultant happiness of that moment when I received it as a prize. Or my Shakespeare, the great Cambridge Shakespeare, it has an odour which carries me yet farther back in life; for these volumes belonged to my father, and before I was old enough to read them with understanding it was often permitted me, as a treat, to take down one of them from the bookcase and reverently to turn the leaves. The volumes smell exactly as they did in that old time, and what a strange tenderness comes upon me when I take one of them in hand!' So true is it that the smell of a thing is the soul of that thing. It is the one vital, essential element about it. The *sight* of a thing may kindle my curiosity; the *sound* of a thing may arouse my interest; but the *smell* of a thing, in some subtle and elusive fashion of its own, avoids all formal avenues of approach and takes possession of all the chambers of my mind at once. I wonder why? Let us get back to the wilds and the woods again!

And here, in the wilds and the woods, let us introduce each other to two of the citizens of that romantic country, men who have been taken into its confidence and initiated into its secrets. Here is Captain C. H. Stigard, a big-game hunter; and here is Frank Buckland, the celebrated naturalist. Let us take the Captain first. He has written a delightful book on *Hunting the Elephant in Africa.* And, oddly enough, he touches on the very point that we have been discussing. 'I believe,' he says, 'I believe the sense of smell is in much more direct connexion with the brain than is the sense of sight. Even with us human beings, who have lost this sense to a great extent, there is nothing like a scent to suddenly and vividly recall forgotten memories. A sound or sight will appear familiar; but the mind will generally have to grope after what it recalls, whilst with a *scent* the memory is an instantaneous flash. Perhaps this, then, is the reason why the duller-witted beast responds so much more quickly and is so much more affected by the sudden noxious smell of a human being than he is by sight.' Now this proves — if it proves no more — that the strange law that operates in man operates no less powerfully among his poorer relations in the field and the forest. And it goes farther. It alleges that the nose is in much more direct communication with the brain than is the eye. And it is at this point that Mr. Buckland comes to our aid, and deals with the same point in greater detail. 'In the head of a deer,' he writes, 'we find three sentinels, which are given to the animal to warn it of danger from its enemies; these sentinels are the nose, the eye, and the ear.' He then proceeds to describe the formation and mechanism of each of these organs, and finishes up by comparing them. 'I place,' he says, 'the organs of sense in the deer's head in the following order of development and use to their owner: 1. The nose. 2. The ear. 3. The eye. These facts may be useful to deer-stalkers, who, if desirous to approach a suspicious deer, should run the chance of the deer seeing them rather than the chance of his hearing them; and, above all, they should avoid all possibility of the deer getting notice of their presence by the *organ of smell.*'

Now all this is very interesting so far as it goes; but, obviously, it does not go far enough. And it is just at the point at which I feel the insufficiency of all these teachers that a still more skilful master comes to my aid. Does the New Testament say nothing about the odours of life? In Dr. Moffatt's fine translation I find Paul speaking of the knowledge of Christ as 'a sweet perfume.' It is a pregnant and suggestive phrase. You would not compare other knowledge to a perfume. But the knowledge of Christ is different. It is intangible, indefinable, inexplicable, inexpressible. You can no more describe it than you can describe the odour of violets. For that matter, you can never describe the best things in life. To a man who has no sense of smell, how would you describe the perfume of roses or boronia or lavender? To a man with no spiritual vision, how would you describe a conversion? A conversion is simply the response of the soul to the 'sweet perfume of Christ,' just as my recollection of my old school was the response of my memory to the perfume of the harrow leaf. I know that, moving along some subtle avenue between my nose and my brain, the odour of that leaf quickened into vigorous life the slumbering faculties of my memory, although I can no more explain how it was done than I can fly. A man need feel, therefore, no sense of shame when he has to confess his inability to explain the potent spell of that lovelier, loftier fragrance.

A Persian fable says: One day
A wanderer found a lump of clay
So redolent of sweet perfume,
Its odour scented all the room.

'Who art thou?' was his quick demand.
'Art thou some gem from Samarkand,
Or spikenard in this rude disguise,
Or other costly merchandise?'

'Nay! I am but a lump of clay.'
'Then whence this wondrous sweetness — say?'
'Friend, if the secret I disclose,
I have been dwelling with the Rose.'

'Wherever I go,' says Paul, 'I scatter the perfume of His knowledge everywhere. I live for God as the fragrance of Christ breathed alike on those who are being saved and on those who are perishing.' I began by saying that this lovely old world of ours is a box of sweetest perfumes. I close by showing that the richest and choicest aroma of them all is diffused, not by scented shrubs or fragrant flowers, but by noble, beautiful, gracious lives.

VIII - Slippers

Slippers, John Broadbanks was telling me, came pretty freely to the manse during the three years that preceded his marriage. When the ladies of Silverstream wished to show their lonely young minister some mark of their appreciation or affection or compassion, it usually took the form of slippers. It is only another instance of that spiritual insight that is one of the principal ingredients in feminine sagacity. They felt, perhaps, in that subconscious or semi-conscious way peculiar to the gentle sex, that there is a subtle but inevitable relationship between the use a man makes of his ministry and the use that he makes of his slippers. I will not go so far as to say that the grace in a man's soul may be measured by the rapidity with which he wears out a pair of slippers; but if anybody else cares to make that daring assertion, I shall not go out of my way to challenge it. Whatever a young wife may forget let her never forget to have the good man's slippers on the fender awaiting his return. If only she can cultivate in him the love of slippers, he will develop into a husband of the finest stamp. The man who is always buying new boots, yet whose slippers last indefinitely, must be regarded with suspicion and distrust. His soul is not quite healthy. Slippery people are an abomination; but slippered people are invariably lovable folk.

A man who wears out plenty of slippers must have an exquisitely tranquil soul. Slippers are such restful things! They look restful; they feel restful; they radiate restfulness among all beholders. I do not know what was in the apostle's mind when he spoke of the feet being shod with the preparation of the gospel of peace; but I know that there is nothing that a man can wear on his feet so expressive of peace as a pair of comfortable slippers. Such a man appears to be on the best of terms with all men in general and with himself in particular; he is the personification of composure, benevolence, and goodwill. A man would only wear slippers in a place that he loves; he would only wear them in the company of people who are dear to him; he would only read under such conditions a book in which his soul delights. In the *Correspondence of Sir Arthur Helps* there appears a letter written to Sir Arthur by Lord Morley. The famous author has sent the great statesman one of his books, and Lord Morley is acknowledging the gift. 'This very night,' he says, 'I shall put on my slippers and dip joyfully into it, and go to bed full of mellow wisdom and goodwill, which is better than anything else. I hold slippers to be a compliment to an author, because who in this easeful fashion would read disagreeable letters or bad books?' Who, indeed? Why, I verily believe that all the best books were written in slippers. It may be fancy, but when I draw my chair up to the fire and put on my slippers and take up some friendly volume that soon fills me with a glow of contentment and delight, I think I can see the pattern of the author's slippers. They are never very bright or showy or new; but they are cosy and faded and loose, and just enough the worse for wear to suggest the constancy of fond familiarity and old friendship.

Give me the man who can look — and feel — perfectly at home in such a pair of slippers! The Autocrat of the Breakfast-table divided men into two classes. There are, he said, men of the cat class and there are men of the *squirrel* class. A squirrel is, for awhile, an engaging companion. It is full of life, overflowing with exuberance and vitality; it is nimble, brisk, and sprightly, leaping over everything and climbing everywhere; it is full of surprises, and astonishes you every second by its agility and its curious antics. But it soon tires you, and you are glad to see it restored to its revolving cage. Similarly, there are people with nimble and restless minds. They are lively, jerky, and smart. Their thoughts do not run in the natural order of sequence. 'They say bright things on all possible subjects, but their zigzags rack you to death. After a jolting half-hour with one of these jerky companions, talking with a dull friend affords great relief. It is like taking the cat in your lap after holding the squirrel!' Just look at the cat lying purring pleasantly on the hearthrug! What could be more restful? And look at the squirrel, already whirling its revolving cage! What could be more restless? Cats and squirrels! To pass from the squirrel-people to the cat-people is, the Autocrat declares, like putting a soft ground-glass shade over a lamp whose naked glare has tortured our tired eyes beyond endurance.

Now, oddly enough, whilst Dr. Oliver Wendell Holmes was writing *The Autocrat* on one side of the Atlantic, Walter Bagehot was penning his famous essays on the other. And, in one of the cleverest of those delightful papers, Bagehot establishes a contrast between stupid people and brilliant people. And, surprising as it may seem, he expresses a decided preference for the former, and argues with resistless force that the world owes incalculably more to people who are stupid than to people who are smart.

But we are getting a long way from home. We set out to talk, not about squirrels, nor about stupidity, but about slippers. Yet we are not so far astray as a casual observer might suppose. For who are the Autocrat's cat-people but the people who can feel perfectly at home in slippers? And who are his squirrel-people but the people who always wear boots? And one has only to read Bagehot's essay a second time in order to see that the contrast at the back of his mind is really the contrast between the people who dearly love a pair of slippers, and the people, who, wearing out cartloads of boots and shoes, yet make a pair of slippers last them half a lifetime.

I referred just now to Silverstream. I think I have already said that I was often a guest at John Broadbanks' manse. It was a pleasant drive from Mosgiel, and we saw a good deal of each other in those days. But I remember well a question that one or other of the children invariably asked at tea-time.

'Is this a "slipper" evening?' somebody would cry.

John's wife saw that I was puzzled when I heard the question for the first time, so she hastened to my enlightenment.

They call it a "slipper" evening,' she explained, 'when John has not to go out. If he has a meeting, they call it a "boot" evening!"

I soon discovered which they liked best.

'Oh, it's a "boot" evening to-night, Don!' he would say, as he rose from the table and went off to prepare for the pending engagement; and every face instantly clouded. But when he announced that it was a 'slipper' evening there were smiles and prancings and clapping of hands. For a 'slipper' evening meant the telling of tales to the little ones and the reading aloud to Myrtle and Jack and mother after the babies were in bed.

I remember one afternoon strolling across the fields behind the manse with John. It was in the early autumn. We sat down in a gap in the gorse hedge and watched the rabbits popping in and out among the tussocks.

'That's a great idea of your youngsters,' I said, 'that distinction between "boot" evening and "slipper" evening!'

'Yes,' he replied, with a laugh, 'and it would astonish you to know the number of books that we get through. Sometimes, even on "boot" nights, I manage to read to them for ten minutes or so before saddling Brownie; on "slipper" nights I read for half an hour, or, if the story is exciting, perhaps a little more. We began with *Pilgrim's Progress.* Then we took *Robinson Crusoe, The Swiss Family Robinson, Uncle Tom's Cabin, Captain Cook's Voyages, Mungo*

Park's Travels, and a few other books of the same kind. During the last year or two we have stuck pretty closely to fiction. It has been great fun, renewing my own acquaintance with Dickens and Scott in the company of the youngsters, and enjoying their excitement on hearing these great stories for the first time.'

He went on to speak of the peals of laughter and glitter of tears that greeted some of the well-known passages in these familiar books.

'Upon my word!' he broke out again, 'it's about the most economical way of being jolly that has ever been invented. About this time last year I had to go into town one day to attend a committee-meeting, and, looking in at the "Chaucer's Head" Bookroom, I picked up a very decent copy of *Pickwick Papers* for a shilling. I brought it home, and, as soon as Myrtle saw the pictures, she made me promise to read it. Night after night, as soon as the teathings were washed up and put away, we all drew our chairs to the fire, and I read one or two, or sometimes three, chapters of Mr. Pickwick's adventures. How we laughed and cried together! We quite pitied the people who, whilst we read, were rushing hither and thither in search of amusement. Here were six of us spending thirty or more evenings crowded with profit and amusement in return for the modest outlay of one single shilling!' And John laughed again, so loudly this time that a pair of rabbits that had been playing unsuspectingly a hundred yards away, dashed instantly to cover.

'Before so very long,' he added reflectively, and with a note of sadness in his voice, 'before so very long the old nest will have to be broken up and all my fledglings will have flown; but I really believe that, long after they have forgotten everything else, they will remember the "slipper" nights that we spent by the fire together!'

And so do I. And this only confirms me in my conviction that the world's best work is done in slippers. When a man takes off his boots and puts on his slippers, he gives you the impression that his work, for the time being, at any rate, is over. But that is only the trickery of appearances. As a matter of fact, when a man takes off his boots and puts on his slippers, his best work is just beginning. John Broadbanks has done a magnificent work at Silverstream, but I doubt if he has done anything finer than the work that he did on his 'slipper' evenings by his own fireside.

History is often made in slippers. Take the case of Sir Joseph Banks. The work that he did in slippers is one of the most extraordinary and unparalleled achievements in the story of the Empire. Joseph Banks accompanied Captain Cook as naturalist on those wonderful and epoch-making voyages that changed the face of the world. But the work even of the greatest navigators must, in the nature of things, be tantalizingly superficial. Cook skirted the coasts of immense continents, but had no time to explore them. Banks stood on the deck of the *Endeavour* and saw the shores of those vast but unknown lands pass, like a panorama, along the horizon, and he vowed that he would dedicate his energies to the work of inspiring young men with a passion for exploration. And most amazingly did he succeed in his self-imposed task. In the days of his retirement, living in his quiet English home, he coaxed young men to his fireside, and, sitting there in his slippers, he told them of the vision of unknown continents that haunted him sleeping and waking. Many of them went back to their homes and offices, smiling superciliously at the old man's enthusiasm. But on the minds of three of his listeners his story had the desired effect. He contrived to fire the fancy, one after the other, of three young men, who, as a result of those fireside conversations, wrote their names in letters indelible upon the world's broad scroll of fame. These three men were Mungo Park, Lachlan Macquarie, and John Franklin. Mungo Park became, under Sir Joseph's influence, the pioneer of African exploration. He began the work that was afterwards completed by Burton, Speke, Livingstone, Stanley, and an army of dauntless and devoted pathfinders. Lachlan Macquarie, also under Sir Joseph's influence, opened the gates of Australia, and converted a microscopic and insignificant settlement into a huge continental dominion. 'I would beg of you,' said Sir Joseph Banks to Colonel Macquarie, on the eve of his sailing for Australia, 'I would beg of you to go out with a strong resolve to open up the country and to discover and develop its resources.' Macquarie came, and, setting himself to the task that Sir Joseph had committed to his trust, the Blue Mountains were soon crossed and the incalculable possibilities of the continent revealed. It was Sir Joseph Banks, too, who inspired Franklin with the idea of opening up the silent seas of the Far North. In 1818 he, being then seventy-five years of age, pleaded with the young naval officer to devote his life to the discovery of the Northwest Passage. The nation being now at peace, he pleaded, some of the most daring and gallant young officers — men who had fought with Nelson at Copenhagen and Trafalgar — might now be commissioned to search for the long-dreamed-of waterway. The nation lent an ear to the old man's plea; young Franklin caught the contagion of the veteran's zeal, and, as a result, and after thirty years' of tireless search, the Northwest Passage was discovered and sealed by the tragic and pathetic sacrifice of its discoverers. Whenever I catch the thrill of African exploration; whenever I feel a glow of admiration as I contemplate the dauntless courage of our Australian pathfinders; whenever I read afresh that stirring record of suffering and adventure in the icy polar seas, I let my mind go one step farther back and I conjure up the image of a stately old gentleman, sitting with slippered feet by a comfortable English fireside. More often than we sometimes think, history is made in slippers.

Thirty or forty years ago the friends of Dr. Alexander Preston issued, as a memorial volume, and for private circulation, a number of autobiographical notes found in the good man's desk after his death. In the second chapter, perhaps the most fascinating in the book. Dr. Preston tells how he found his way to faith and to the ministry. 'I owe my soul,' he says, 'to no preacher or teacher. I was born in the tiny village of Cudford Brook, and down a little lane that ran from the village green to the brook itself there stood a pretty old cottage. In the summer-time the porch was a tangle of roses. The door, even in winter, always stood open; and nobody who knew Old Duncan, as we called him, ever thought of knocking. We walked right in, and he was always pleased. He sat by his fire, a little old gentleman in slippers; and, even as a small boy, I revelled in his company. He was interested in all my games and my lessons, and he always knew what I ought to do. If I was puzzled or disappointed, I always went and told Old Duncan. He seemed to understand boys. And he used at times to speak to me about the kingdom of heaven. And, somehow, he made it wonderfully attractive. He always took it for granted that I should love his Saviour, and his Bible, and his church, and all the things that were so dear to him. "When you are a minister of the Word, Sandy," he would say; and he made me feel that that was part of the divine programme; and, surely enough, it has all come to pass exactly as he said!' And, later on, Preston refers again to Old Duncan: 'The red carpet slippers,' he says, 'seemed a part of him. And when he died nobody had the heart to burn them; so they put them where they had almost always been, and in his slippers he was buried!'

'A little old gentleman in slippers!' We are all moving towards the sovereignty of the slippers. Life itself is a march towards slippers. Happy they who have caught the restful spirit of the slippers, to whom the slippers represent not an imprisonment, but — as in the case of Joseph Banks and Old Duncan — the opportunity for a radiant sunset ministry.

IX - The Miser of Murdstone Creek

For nearly an hour we had seen no sign of human habitation. We were motoring along one of our great Australian highroads, and the dense bush ran riot everywhere. All at once we saw, right ahead of us, a little old man, with long, shaggy beard, leaning heavily on a stick. He had evidently emerged from the bush on our right, and was leisurely crossing the road. He moved slowly and painfully until he reached the centre of the highway. At that moment he heard, for the first time, the throbbing of the car. He paused, glanced furtively towards us, and then, startled and terrified, he shambled on as quickly as he could go, diving into the thick scrub on our left. When we reached the spot we pulled up, but could see no sign of him. A couple of miles farther on we came upon the little township of Murdstone, nestling among the foothills of the Western Tiers. In ordering some refreshment we reported what we had seen.

'Oh, that was nothing,' replied the good woman, as she went on laying the cloth for our entertainment. 'That was Old Father Grab, as the boys call him, the Miser of Murdstone Creek. He lives in a hollow tree down the gully, near the stream. He hates to be seen by anybody. It is a wonder that he allowed you to catch sight of him. You must have come quickly round the bend after he had got out into the open.'

An hour later we had left Murdstone and its miser a long way behind us, and the matter slipped from our remembrance. But, somehow, it has rushed back upon my mind this evening.

The miser is a model for us all. I know, of course, that it is considered correct to vilify and malign him. But that is nothing to go by. The crowd often crucifies those whom it should crown, and crowns those whom it should crucify. These things go by fashion. Near a large public school I saw the other day a group of boys, just released from their tasks. One of them espied a sparrow sitting on a paling-fence fifty yards away. Instantly he stooped, seized a stone, and threw it at the bird. A second boy followed suit. Then another and another, until, before the bird took wing, almost the entire group was engaged in throwing stones at the sparrow. In the same way somebody once threw a stone at the miser. Somebody else followed, and so on, until now it is considered quite the correct thing to say the bitterest things that can possibly be said about this unhappy man.

'I have seen a good deal of misers,' says the Poet at the Breakfast-table, 'and I think I understand them as well as most people do.' Indeed, he became an amateur miser himself. He tells us in another place that he once kept a little gold by him in order to ascertain the exact amount of pleasure to be got out of handling it. And, as a result, his eyes were opened, and he said hard things about the miser no more. 'I understand now,' he says, 'the delight that an old ragged wretch, starving himself in a crazy hovel, takes in stuffing guineas into old stockings and filling earthen pots with sovereigns, and every now and then visiting his hoards and fingering the fat pieces, and thinking over all that they represent of earthly and angelic and diabolic energy. A miser pouring out his guineas into his palm, and bathing his shrivelled and trembling hands in the yellow heaps before him, is not the prosaic being we are in the habit of thinking him. He is a dreamer, almost a poet. Think of the significance of the symbols he is handling!' Symbols! Symbols of what?

'Symbols of Power, to be sure!' answers Sir Walter Scott; for, in *The Fair Maid of Perth,* Sir Walter has given us a miser. His name is Henbane Dwining, the apothecary. Hear him in his own defence! 'Henbane Dwining,' he says, as he gazes in delight upon the hoards which he has secretly amassed, and which he visits whenever the fancy takes him, 'Henbane Dwining is no silly miser, doting on pieces for their golden lustre; it is the power with which they endow the possessor which makes him thus adore them.' And he chuckles over the reflection that the smile of beauty, the dagger of revenge, the intoxication of pleasure, the control of fields of fair flowers and forests of rich game, the favour of courts, the honours of kings, the pardon of popes, are all, through their virtue, at his beck and call!

'Yes, symbols, and symbols of Power!' says the Poet. 'The contents of that old glove will buy him the willing service of many an adroit sinner, and with what that coarse sack contains he can purchase the prayers of holy men for all succeeding time. In this chest is a castle in Spain, a real one, and not only in Spain, but anywhere he will choose to have it. All these things, and a thousand more, the miser hears and sees and feels and hugs and enjoys as he paddles with his lean hands among the sliding, shining, ringing, innocent-looking bits of yellow metal, toying with them as the lion-tamer handles the great carnivorous monster, whose might and whose terrors are child's play to the latent forces and power of harm-doing of the glittering counters played with in the great game between angels and devils.' I must apologize for having detained the Poet so long, but I am most anxious to set the miser in a pleasant light before the eyes of my reader; and nothing is more likely to brush away any old prejudices that that reader may cherish than the eloquent testimony I have just quoted.

The miser is guided by a true instinct. It is right to hoard. The only mistake that the miser makes, and it is a mere matter of detail, is that he hoards the wrong things. He hoards gold, and gold is not to be despised. But there are things better worth hoarding even than gold; and the miser who is really an adept at the game will quickly find them out. I have just been reading the biography of Miss Annie J. Clough, the famous Principal of Newnham College, and one of the pioneers of our modern educational system. It is a beautiful and noble life. But I was impressed by the insistence with which Miss Clough urged upon the young ladies under her charge the importance of storing the mind in youth with beautiful memories. The average person can, she insisted, furnish himself with experiences that, costing neither time nor money, will nevertheless yield infinite satisfaction when seen in the retrospect of the years. Miss Clough reminds me of Henry Ryecroft. Lovers of George Gissing will remember that when Ryecroft realized, in the days of age and infirmity, the exquisite pleasure afforded him by the recollection of youthful strolls in the fir copse, in the primrosed woods, in the poppy-sprinkled cornfields, and in the meadows full of buttercups, he was filled with remorse at the reflection that he had spent so much of his time amidst conditions that provided him with no such pleasing retrospect. I remember once chatting with a man who had lost his sight in a colliery explosion. He was telling me that, every day of his life, there rushes back to mind some little thing that caught his eye in the old days. The squirrel that he saw in the beech-trees; the daisychain that his sister made as they sat together in the summer fields; the column of spray that dashed skywards when the waves broke against the cliffs; the swallow that he watched as it skimmed the surface of the millpond and returned with a captured fly to the nest under the eaves; the bare branches in the forest bowed down with their heavy freight of snow; the glow of sunset; the grey of dawn; the glimmer of twilight; the merry twinkle of a boy's eye; the soft crimson of a girl's blush — he could never express his gratitude that his mind was stored with thousands of such images.

I have no stones to throw at the miser. I am sorry for him. The boys at Murdstone called him 'Old Father Grab,' whilst my hostess at the refreshment-rooms called him the 'Miser of Murdstone Creek.' And, on the whole, her name for him is more pathetic than their nickname. In his great chapter 'On the Morality in Words' Archbishop Trench instances the word 'miser' as a distinguished example of a word having in its very composition an attestation of eternal truth. The words 'miser' and 'misery' come, the Archbishop shows, from the same root. 'Is it strange, then,' he asks, 'that men should have agreed to call him a miser, or miserable, who eagerly scrapes together and painfully hoards the mammon of this world? By calling such a man a "miser" the moral instinct lying deep in all hearts has borne testimony to the tormenting nature of this vice; to the gnawing pains with which even in his present time it punishes its votaries; to the enmity which exists between it and all joy. The man who enslaves himself to his money is proclaimed in our very language to be a "miser" or miserable man.' Here, therefore, we have one of those rare cases in which the name is truer and more expressive than the nickname.

'Old Father Grab!' cried the boys of the township; and there was derision and resentment in their cry.

'The Miser of Murdstone Creek!' said our hostess at the tea-rooms; and in her more exact description there was an undertone of tears.

George Eliot, in introducing us to Silas Marner, the miser of Raveloe, discusses with us, in her pleasant way, the miser's singular passion. She thinks that it arises from our human love of completing sets of things. Let her state her theory in her own way. 'Have not men, shut up in solitary confinement, found an interest in marking the moments by straight strokes of a certain length on the wall, until the growth of the sum of straight strokes, arranged in triangles, has become a mastering purpose? Do we not wile away moments of inanity or fatigued waiting by repeating some trivial movement or sound, until the repetition has bred a want, which is incipient habit? That will help us to understand how the love of accumulating money grows into an absorbing passion. Marner wanted the heaps of ten to grow into a square; and then into a larger square; and every added guinea, while it was itself a satisfaction, bred a new desire.' We like to complete a score; and then a hundred; and then a thousand; and then a million. Every cricketer knows what I mean. How he loves to complete a century! To be bowled at ninety-nine is an exasperating experience. The difference between ninety-eight and ninety-nine is a difference of one; but the difference between ninety-nine and a hundred is enormous!

I am sorry for the miser, too, because his hoard does not increase automatically, as it would do if he entrusted it to a banker. It does not, like old wine, improve with age. It is at this point that the memory has the advantage of the miser. When the miser goes to the old stocking in which he stored five hundred sovereigns, he finds five hundred sovereigns there: they are sovereigns still, and there are just five hundred of them. But when, after a period of time, you go to the memory, you find what was once a very little thing; but to what a great thing has it grown! The buttercups in the fields of childhood have become part of life's most precious hoard. Or look at this!

'Good-bye, Steer forth,' said David Copperfield, as he looked into the face of his friend for the last time, 'good-bye!'

'He was unwilling to let me go,' says David, 'and stood, holding me, with a hand on each of my shoulders.'

'Good-bye!' he said at last, 'and, Davie, if anything should ever separate us, you must think of me at my best, old boy. Come! Let us make that bargain. Think of me at my best, if circumstances should ever part us.'

They parted; and Davie never saw Steerforth again till he saw his face up-turned in death, tossed ashore by the waves after the storm and the ship-wreck.

'*Think of me at my best*'; it is one of the deepest of our human cravings. And it is the charm of that secret hoard that memory treasures that it answers to that passionate yearning. For our memories are the most charitable and kindly things about us. The memory is rarely guilty of harsh judgment or of slander; she speaks well of almost everything and everybody. She accentu-ates the pleasurableness of pleasure, making many things much more attrac-tive in retrospect than they seemed in reality. She robs pain of much that is revolting. Like the ivy that creeps over the crumbling ruin and imparts a beauty to deformity, the trying and exasperating things of life are made to appear romantic or humorous as we tell the story years afterwards. 'Noth-ing,' says a great American, 'can be so perfect while we possess it as it will seem when remembered. The friend we love best may sometimes weary us by his presence, or vex us by his infirmities. How sweet to think of him as he will be to us after we have outlived him ten or a dozen years!' Memory thus contrives to see the most mundane and unalluring objects through a kind of golden haze. The miser's pence never by any chance turn into pounds; but in the memory all our geese become swans.

But most of all am I sorry for the miser because he is always oppressed by the limitations of his wealth. He always has one pile that is incomplete; and it vexes him. It makes him miserable — a miser! I could not help thinking of the Miser of Murdstone Creek yesterday when I was preparing to preiach on the '*unsearchable riches.*' I was struck by the various translations. Dr. Weymouth speaks of the '*exhaustless* wealth' of Christ; Dr. Moffatt renders it '*fathomless* wealth'; whilst Dr. Jowett tells a story. 'Once,' he says, 'I heard Dr. Rendel Harris read the chapter in which these words are found, and he read from his pocket Greek Testament, and gave his own translation. And I remember how, when he came to this passage, he threw out his arms in a wide gesture as he repeated the words "the *unexplorable* wealth of Christ." We had a suggestion of a vast continent, not yet tracked out, with roads only here and there.' Now here is a collection!

'*Unsearchable riches!*' say the Authorized and Revised Versions, with a thought of the height and mystery of this invisible treasure.

'*Exhaustless wealth!*' says Dr. Weymouth, with a hint at its everlasting dura-tion.

'*Fathomless wealth!*' says Dr. Moffatt, with a suggestion of immeasurable profundities and unplumbed depths.

'*Unexplorable wealth!*' says Dr. Rendel Harris, as he thinks of its continental breadths and uncharted immensities.

Let us hope that some home missionary or bush evangelist will look in at the hollow tree down the gully and make the old miser's eyes to sparkle as he unfolds such astonishing and unsuspected treasure!

X - The Secret

A SECRET is a maddening affair. It goads and stings without discrimination and without pity. It tortures, like a grand inquisitor, both the man who possesses and the man who covets it. The one is bursting to tell his secret; the other is burning to know it. The one is like a bottle filled with highly effervescent fluid tightly corked; the other is like a bottle empty and ashamed. But look at this. They were off to school, side by side, Jessie and Joan.

'Do tell me!' pleaded Jessie.

'But I promised I would tell nobody,' explained Joan.

And so, all through the long school-morning, two little lassies, usually bright as sunshine, bent over their tasks with faces clouded and glum. The secret was a kill-joy. It had spoiled all the fun for both of them.

The worst of it is that secrets are such noisy things. If a man carries a sovereign in his pocket, he keeps it dark. Nobody knows it. He does not proclaim it from the housetops for ^he information of every thieves' kitchen. But with a secret it is otherwise. A secret is more coveted than a sovereign. Yet, by an odd perversity, the man who carries a secret lets all the world know that he carries it. You can see it in his eyes; you can detect it in his behaviour; you may even hear it from his lips. He does not, of course, tell you the secret itself; but he exasperates you by confiding to you the fact that he holds a secret. That is why it is so much more easy to pick a man's brains of secrets than to pick his pockets of sovereigns.

Take Cabinet Ministers, for example. I have been reading Dasent's great *Life of Delane.* When Delane edited *The Times,* there were no such things as Cabinet secrets. Delane wouldn't allow them! The Czar of Russia read the British ultimatum in *The Times* before he received the document from the British ambassador! No decision of any importance was reached by Her Majesty's advisers but *The Times* published it before the responsible Minister had had time to announce it! Every new appointment appeared first in the paper, and was afterwards communicated to Parliament! Premiers stormed; Ministers thundered; members made angry speeches; officials complained bitterly; but still the conditions knew no change. Lord Derby, in the Upper House, almost demanded the head of the offender. Where was the leakage? Who supplied the information? 'A cask,' remarked Lord Malmesbury, 'may leak just as easily at the top as at the bottom,' and conscience-stricken Ministers looked at each other in amazement or guiltily hung their heads. The journalists knew all the moves in the game. The clubs had a story of one noble lord whose face always assumed a look of extraordinary importance when a Cabinet secret was tucked away among the cerebral convolutions of his brain. A certain reporter, who made it his business to scrutinize his lordship's countenance closely, knew that look well. He pounced upon his prey like a fox on a goose.

'Well, my lord,' he would say, quite casually, 'so you have settled such-and-such a matter at last!'

His lordship would look astonished, and concluded that the official announcement must have been made, or else that some other member of the Cabinet had been less discreet than himself.

'Yes,' he would reply, 'and, since you know so much, there can be no harm in telling you the rest!'

And so it came about that at daylight the paper appeared with the whole story!

Now and then it may' happen that a Cabinet Minister is relieved of a sovereign that he was carrying in his pocket. But that is only now and again, because sovereigns are so silent. Cabinet Ministers do not advertise the fact that they carry sovereigns in their pockets. But every day Cabinet Ministers are relieved of the secrets that they carry in their minds. For, unlike the sovereigns, secrets are so noisy. The man who carries a secret proclaims to all the world that he carries that secret. And, as a natural result, the secret is very soon a secret no longer.

A secret, as I have said, is a maddening affair. It teases and tantalizes and taunts me. Be I young or old, male or female, I am aflame with curiosity and busy with inquisitive investigations until I know all about it, and then, in all probability, I laugh at myself for having bothered my head about such a stupid or trivial matter. But, meanwhile, the time has come to pull ourselves up and ask ourselves a particularly plain and pertinent question. Is a secret a good thing or a bad thing? Is it a good thing or a bad thing that, as soon as Jessie discovers that Joan has a secret, poor little Jessie can think of nothing else until she has solved the captivating mystery? Is it a good thing or a bad thing that, as soon as Fleet Street gets wind of a secret in Downing Street, an army of journalists, keen as hounds on the scent, give Cabinet Ministers no rest night or day until they have run their quarry to earth? Is it a good thing or a bad thing that, as soon as I find that my neighbour holds a secret, I am wretched and ill at ease until I too am in possession of it? It is a good thing; unquestionably a good thing. I am prepared to argue that the secrets of the world have been the salvation of the world.

What is the eternal quest for knowledge but the response of our tantalized minds to the taunting secrets of the universe?

Twinkle, twinkle, little star!
How I wonder what you are!
Up above the world so high,
Like a diamond in the sky.

There was the question — a question asked, in that form or in some other, by the first inhabitants of this planet. And the longer that question remained unanswered, the more restless men became. The stars; the secrets of the stars; what were the secrets of the stars? And out of that insatiable hunger for a secret, astrology and astronomy were born. Had a secret possessed no power to inflame the curiosity of men, we should never have had a Copernicus, a Galileo, a Kepler, a Newton, a Herschel. Because the silence of the skies was more than man could bear, he set to work to wrest their story from them. The Tower of Babel was the germ from which the Greenwich Observatory evolved. And so man came at length to know the sun and moon, Jupiter and Saturn, as well as London knows Melbourne or Melbourne Hong Kong. The same is true of the strata beneath our feet. The silence of the past was a terrible thing. What had happened on this planet before we arrived here — before our history books began? Here was a secret for you! And that secret teased the imagination of man, until he set to work to dig up the records.

With what frenzy of eager enthusiasm he searched for that secret! No prospector hunting after gold at Klondyke or Calgoorlie ever tore up the earth with fiercer zest. His pickaxe shook the planet.

> Beneath the seas he made a stair;
> He laid the primal forges bare;
>   He asked if Truth were hid
>   'Neath cairn or pyramid;
>   He questioned rune and kann,
>   And bones as old as man.

And thus, in that passionate quest of a secret, the science of geology was born! And what means all this romantic tale of exploration — these bronzed travellers back from the interior of great continents, these battered ships back from the Poles? It is the same old story. There were secrets! How the secret as to the fountains of the Nile taunted the brain of Livingstone! In the delirium of death he was still babbling of the fountains, the unseen fountains. How the secret of the West tantalized the fancy of Columbus! How the secrets of the snows have lured to their triumphs a great host of Arctic and Antarctic adventurers! If science is a good thing, it follows that a secret is a good thing; for if the world had been challenged by no secrets, it would certainly have been enriched by no science.

No man's equipment is complete unless he is furnished with a fair stock of secrets. The man who can air all his knowledge to everybody knows nothing worth imparting to anybody. A man's wealth must be measured, not by what he pays away, but what he still possesses after all his obligations are discharged. A water-supply must be measured, not by the flow at the tap, but by the depth and fullness of the reservoir. And, similarly, a man's knowledge must be gauged, not by his conversation, but by his reserves. A wise man knows more than he ever tells. He may share much of his knowledge with the multitude; he may divide some of his best things among his intimates and companions; he may keep a few of his priceless treasures for the wife of his bosom; but, even then, he will reserve a few choice morsels for himself and for himself alone. Like a gardener who feels that he must himself taste some of the choicest fruit he grows, like a miser who runs his fingers through his hoard in secret, the wise man has a few things that are strictly and solely for his own delectation.

There is something very impressive about a dignified reticence. The Scotsman of the true type never carries his heart on his sleeve. The English gentleman of the old school is very conservative in the selection of his friends. It is a bad sign when a man becomes prodigal of his secrets. When he feels that he must take everybody into his confidence, and tell everybody everything, he should instantly send for a doctor. He is getting morbid. A man is never so poor as when his stock of secrets has run low. For the matter of that, it is a bad sign when a nation becomes garrulous and talks about everything. There are some subjects that are too sacred to be exposed to the glare of the footlights. They do not fit the flicker of a film. They are too majestic to be bandied to and fro in the course of a newspaper controversy. Humanity has a few secrets; and, when humanity is quite healthy and sane, it does not drag those secrets on to the stage or discuss them in the press. There is something wrong somewhere when a people is prepared to talk about everything.

Religion in itself is essentially a matter of secrets. Emerson, writing of his visit to England, said that no man could understand England or English history unless he were in the secret. And the secret of England, he maintained, was England's faith. 'That divine secret,' he goes on to say, 'has existed in England from the days of Alfred the Great to those of Florence Nightingale.' A divine secret, mark you! That is the mistake that they make who seek to penetrate the superb silences of revelation. Of the life beyond the grave, for instance, the Scriptures speak with sublime and awful reticence. As against this, we have the grotesque history of seances and table-rappings. 'These records,' says Mr. Augustine Birrell, until recently one of His Majesty's advisers, 'these records leave me unconvinced. They lack grandeur. They deal with petty things. A revelation of a life beyond the grave ought surely to be more stupendous than that — something of really first-class importance. Otherwise we are just as well without it.' Precisely! Even God is entitled to His secrets. There are things about which inspiration can afford to be silent. The fact before which Pompey stood bewildered when he burst into the Holy of Holies was the awful stillness of the place. No priest spake; no choir chanted; the Temple was invaded, but it held its secrets still. A stately reticence is infinitely nobler than an ignominious speech.

The soul itself is essentially a secret thing. It does not advertise itself as the body does. It loathes the limelight. It dreads publicity. It shrinks from the glare. The deepest things can never be told. 'He told me all things that ever I did,' said the woman of Samaria to her fellow townsmen. That is a masterpiece of Revelation and of Reticence. She did not say what those things were. She did not glory in her own shame. She revealed all that it was needful to reveal; she concealed all that it was womanly to conceal. The man who can reveal to his fellows the whole of his religious experience has no experience worth revealing. Faith, to quote Newman's fine phrase, has large reserves. The Old Testament likens the growth of the soul to the growth of a tree. Oliver Wendell Holmes used to say that a tree is a most wonderful creature standing on its head. The principal part is underground. Those marvellous fibres that scent their food and water from afar, and that accomplish the most astounding engineering feats in order to reach it, are all stowed away in the darkness. What the tree displays is as nothing to what the tree hides. The New Testament likens the relationship existing between the soul and its Saviour to the relationship existing between a bride and her bridegroom. A proud young wife may draw aside the veil in order to permit her bosom friends to peep for a moment at her felicity; but what she reveals is as nothing to what she conceals. Like the tree, the soul draws her sustenance from darkest depths and hidden springs; she lives on her secrets. Like the bride, the soul derives her satisfaction from a holy and beautiful relationship, the mystic character of which no tongue can ever tell.

XI - Mary Golding

I CANNOT think of Mary Golding without feeling heartily ashamed of myself. Captain Stuart and Major Mitchell, when they were blazing our great Australian trails, crossed the districts that were afterwards riddled with diggings, and never so much as noticed the gold strewn everywhere about them! The wheels of their bullock-drays crushed through the quartz; yet the thought of the precious metal never once occurred to them. We all go through life in pretty much the same way. For some years I must have bustled past the buxom, good-humoured figure of old Mary Golding twice every day without dreaming that I was so near to the fringe of a great romance. It is part of the pathos of this pathetic old world that we are not introduced to many of the people best worth knowing until after they have dropped into their graves. Mary Golding has just dropped into hers. For sixty years she sold newspapers every day at the corner of Northumberland Avenue and Whitehall. Indeed, Mary took over the pitch from her mother; so that, mother and daughter, the pair of them had been selling papers on that selfsame spot for the biggest part of a century. Very few of those whose business now takes them to Charing Cross will be able to recall the elder lady; but millions of us must have brushed past Mary Golding without even noticing her. In all weathers, we are told, Mary Golding was at her post. Last December, as she was turning her face towards home after selling her last paper, she was knocked violently down by a passing taxi, but she limped back to her place

49

next morning. The severe winter has, however, proved too much for her, and the place that has known her for sixty years will know her no more. The London papers, with whose circulation the old lady was so closely identified, noticed her death, and even expressed regret; but there is something about such a career that appeals to the imagination. As a mark of respect, and in token of my sorrow at having passed her so often without even raising my hat to her, I propose to indulge in a little speculation.

Like the cloud of sparrows that rises into the air as you approach a ripening cornfield, a whole host of questions is started by the thought of Mary Golding. And to think that I might have asked those questions and received from her own lips the answers! But I will ask them still, and the silence that follows shall be my just rebuke and fitting retribution. For one would like to know more about the old newsvender, and especially about the way in which she regarded her work. There is room for a good deal of psychological conjecture. Did she look upon it as a mere matter of rote — everlastingly dealing out papers in return for pennies and halfpennies? It is conceivable that she may have felt herself to be almost as mechanical as the penny-inthe-slot machines. The boys, flying hither and thither, experience the thrill of rivalry, almost the excitement of the chase, as they watch with eager eyes for possible customers, and dart in and out amidst the traffic in their haste to effect a sale. But Mary Golding had but to stand still, and she may have felt that the perpetual handing out of papers in return for coppers converted her into the merest piece of mechanism to which humanity can be reduced. As she stood there day after day she saw men and women come dancing past her with bright eyes and flushed faces. She could see that their lives were all novelty and excitement. But she saw also hundreds of creatures who came every day at exactly the same time, who approached every day at exactly the same pace, who wore every day exactly the same expression, and who were going every day to exactly the same tasks.

There was a boy who was on his way to a factory to stick endless piles of labels on endless rows of pots. There was a girl who was hurrying to a restaurant to stand all day behind a curtain washing up a pile of dirty dishes. There, on the poor girl's left, stood the greasy plates; and there, on her right, stood those that she had cleaned. But the pile on her left never grew any smaller, and the pile on her right never grew any taller, because the hands of the waitresses, like the phantom hands of fate, darted in and out of the curtains, everlastingly adding to the one pile and everlastingly subtracting from the other. From morning till night she washed and washed and washed; but the pile of dirty plates was like the widow's cruse, it never wasted away. Then there was a woman with a hunted look in her eye, who passed Mary Golding every morning at precisely eleven minutes past eight. She was on her way to sew buttons of one unvarying kind on garments of one unvarying pattern. And then there was Clark. I feel sure that Clark passed Mary Golding on his way to the office in Fleet Street. Mark Rutherford has made us all familiar with Clark. He was an address-copier. 'The monotony of that perpetual address-copying was terrible. He has told me with a kind of shame what an effect it had upon him, that sometimes for days he would feed upon the prospect of the most childish trifle because it would break in some slight degree the uniformity of his toil. For example, he would sometimes change from quill to steel pens and back again, and he found himself actually looking forward with a kind of joy — merely because of the variation — to the day on which he had fixed to go back to the quill after using steel.' These people Mary saw go past her every day like creatures on a treadmill. And, as she thought of herself, standing at the same spot, doling out everlasting papers in return for everlasting pennies, it may be that she felt that she was the most mechanical puppet of them all.

It may be. But then again, it is at least equally possible that she caught something of the romance of the thing. There is a piquant pleasure that only the gossip knows. The joy of having something to tell that everybody else is dying to hear is one of the wildest delights of which some natures are capable. Did Mary Golding feel, as she handed out her papers, that that rapture was her perpetual bliss? She was only a child when, in 1857, she took her mother's place. The year 1857 was a very notable one. It was the year of the Indian Mutiny. London was hungry for the latest news. The girl may be pardoned if she took a peculiar and personal pleasure in spreading the thrilling items as soon as they were available. One of the first papers that she sold told of the Relief of Lucknow.

Dance to the pibroch! — saved! We are saved! is it you?
Is it you?
Saved by the valour of Havelock, saved by the blessing of Heaven!
'Hold it for fifteen days I' We have held it for eighty-seven!
And ever aloft on the palace roof the banner of England blew!

Then, again, 1857 was David Livingstone's great year in England. Did the romance of the African wilds enter into the soul of Mary Golding that year? A girl would be unusually apathetic and stolid who found no delight in handing out papers that told such tidings to the eager and anxious men as they passed to and fro. And if, in those early days of her business, she imbibed such a temper, it is possible that all the drama of subsequent history wove itself into her spirit, and she felt herself to be part and parcel of every stirring movement of which her papers told. The more I think about it, the more do I wish that I had noticed and spoken to her in my old London days. Through her soul the pageant of empires may have swept. Kings, councils, and continents may have been the commonplaces of her thought. Mary Golding may have converted her newspaper pitch at the street-corner into an observatory from which she every hour surveyed the universe.

And, talking of that long stand of hers at the street-corner, it would be interesting to know whether, in the course of those sixty years, Mary ever sighed for a change of scene. Did she not sometimes fancy that she would like to exchange pitches with some newsvender at Kensington or Regent Street? But here, again, there are two strangely divergent possibilities. It is conceivable, on the one hand, that, as the years went by, she grew sick of the thought of Northumberland House, and only trudged back to the old spot, in sunshine or in snow, in summer and in winter, under the remorseless pressure of a cruel necessity. Could anything be more wearisomely monotonous than to spend one's whole day, from dawn to dark, year in and year out, without holiday or relief, at the same spot for sixty long years? And yet, on the other hand, it is at least equally possible that, with the years, she fell in love with the place, and felt that she could not live without it. We grow to things, like the ivy to the wall. Richard Jefferies was once asked why he walked the same road every day. The question startled him, and he could not immediately answer it. It had never occurred to him that he *had* adhered so closely to the same path. 'Not till years afterwards,' he says, 'was I able to see why I went the same round and why I did not care for change. I do not want change; I want the same old and loved things. I want the same wild flowers, the same trees, the same soft ash-green! I want the same turtle-doves, the same blackbirds, the same coloured yellowhammer, singing, so long as there is light enough to cast a shadow on the dial, the same old song! And I want them all in the same places! Let me see the idle shadows resting on the white dust; let me hear the humble-bees, and stay to look down on the dandelion disc; let me see the chaffinch with a feather in her bill! No change for me! Let me see the same things on the same road, keeping the same succession year by year!'

I recognize, in quoting Richard Jefferies, that there is a vast difference between a Sussex lane and a London street-corner. But it is just as possible to lose one's heart to a city pavement as to a country pasture. We get fond of things, not because of their intrinsic beauty, but because of our very familiarity with them. They become part of us, and we of them. What about Tim Linkinwater? 'It's forty-four year,' said poor Tim, when it was proposed to give him some relief from his regular duties, 'it's forty-four year next May since I first kept the books of Cherryble Brothers. I've opened the safe every morning all that time as the clock struck nine, and gone over the house every night at half -past ten to see the doors fastened and the fires out. I've never slept out of the back attic one single night. There's the same mignonette box in the middle of the window, and the same four flowerpots, two on each side, that I brought with me when I first came. There ain't — I've said it again and again, and I'll maintain it — there ain't such a square as this in the world; not one. For business or pleasure, in summer-time or winter — I don't care which — there's nothing like it. There's not such a spring in England as the pump under the archway. There's not such a view in England as the view out of my window; I've seen it every morning before I shaved, and I ought to know something about it. I have slept in that room for forty-four year, and if it wasn't inconvenient and didn't interfere with business, I should request leave to die there!' Dickens knew, when he drew Tim Linkinwater, that he was painting from life. I like to fancy that Mary Golding entertained the same agreeable sentiments concerning the street-corner at which so much of her life was passed.

Moreover, Mary Golding had one immense advantage over Tim Linkinwater, inasmuch as the personal element entered more largely into her life. A street-corner is alive with personal interest. There are the people who come past every day, and who come past at exactly the same time. There are the people who come frequently, but whose coming is irregular and erratic. And there are the strangers. Mary Golding would probably only welcome the members of this latter class as imparting a tinge of variety and novelty to her ordinary outlook. Her delight would be in the regular comers. A man would pass her four times a day for twenty years without exchanging a word, yet if, on any one occasion, he were ten minutes late, the circumstance would awaken her interest; and, if he absented himself altogether, she would await the next day with impatience and concern. She may have fancied, and with some justice, that this silent interest was reciprocal. In her time she regularly sold her papers to Lord Salisbury, to Lord Hartington, to Mr. John Burns, and to Mr. Gladstone. If ever a heavy cold or a twinge of rheumatism suggested the advisability of a day at home, it is quite on the cards that the good woman flattered herself that, were she to yield to such a temptation, Mr. Gladstone would be wondering what had become of her. Life has an amiable habit of flattering us in this particular, and of wedding us to our work. However modest our duties may be, we get into the way, after a number of years, of fancying that things could not go on without us. Mary Golding may quite easily have schooled herself into believing that Northumberland House would have to close its doors unless she stood just outside the gate with her papers. No item of news upon her placards, she would fancy, could be quite so astounding and sensational as her own disappearance from the familiar spot.

It is by whispering such things into our ears that life binds us to our allotted tasks, and renders attractive to us duties that, to an outsider, might seem repugnant and intolerable. Sour-visaged philosophers may tell us if they will that no man is indispensable; but, as a matter of actual fact, we all meet life every morning with a smile and a song because in our hearts we believe that the world could not get on without us. Something whispers it to us, and, in spite of the philosophers, we all believe it; and, because we all believe it, the work of the world gets done.

Part Two

I - Drifting Apart

We were sitting on the cliffs at Beechington, reading. At least, we were co-quetting with our books, for one's attention is always divided, under such conditions, between the volume on his knee and the broad expanse of blue water that stretches out before him. In the distance we could see the heads. All at once a fine steamer crept out from between the great rugged promontories, and put out to sea. To our surprise, it was followed almost immediately by another. It may have been owing to the light and atmospheric conditions, but, from where we sat, the two ships looked as much alike as two peas in a pod. Indeed, one could almost imagine that he was gazing upon a mirage, and that the one was really but a reflection of the other. One behind the other, the two vessels crept along the skyline as though the one had the other in tow. Then came the change. One swerved slightly to port, and the other slightly to starboard. We turned once more to our books. And when we looked up again, the alteration was almost incredible. The one ship, having come nearer, looked immensely larger; the other was a mere speck on the horizon. The one was still in the sunshine; the other was shaded by a passing cloud. The two appeared to have nothing in common. It seemed impossible that, half an hour ago, they had been so near together and looked so much alike. Here, surely, was an allegory. I was gazing at a picture of the things that drift apart.

I

I thought of Abraham and Lot. Abraham and Lot journeyed together all the way from the Persian Gulf to Palestine; from Palestine to the Pyramids; and were on their way to Palestine again. Then they drifted apart. *'There was strife between the herdmen of Abraham's cattle and the herdmen of Lot's cattle. And Abraham, said unto Lot, Let there be no strife, I pray thee, between me and thee, and between my herdmen and thy herdmen; for we are brethren. Is not the whole land before thee? Separate thyself, I pray thee, from me. If thou wilt take the left hand, I will go to the right; and if thou wilt take the right hand, I will go to the left. And Lot chose him all the Plain of Jordan; and Lot journeyed east: and they separated themselves the one from the other.'* Anybody who afterwards saw Abraham with his tent pitched, and his altar built, on the plains of Mamre, and Lot with his tent pitched towards Sodom, and with no altar at all, would never have dreamed that, once upon a time, they journeyed so closely together and seemed so much alike. I thought of this story, I say, as I watched the two ships from the cliffs at Beechington.

II

There is an essential difference between two and a pair, A sovereign and a sixpenny-bit are two, the fox and the goose are two, the hare and the tortoise are two; you cannot arrange these in pairs. Christian and Pliable are two; they go side by side, but all eternity lies between them. Christian and Faithful, on the other hand, are a pair; they may be torn from each other's embrace, but all eternity cannot really separate them. John and Judas are two; David and Jonathan are a pair. Proximity is no indication of affinity. More than a century ago two men voyaged together round the coast of Scotland. Anybody looking at them from the shore would have supposed that they were a pair. They were nothing of the kind; they were two. One was Robert Stevenson, Engineer to the Board of Northern Lighthouses; the other was Sir Walter Scott. But, although they share the same boat, they have scarcely anything in common. Scott loves the fair weather; Stevenson the foul. Scott likes to get ashore, wander up over the hills, inspect some crumbling old ruin, get among the gossips of the countryside and gather up those quaint old legends and stirring traditions that he will afterwards weave into his great romances. Stevenson, on the other hand, is thinking, not of the past, but of the future. His eye is not on castles that have been, but on lighthouses yet to be. He loves to see the ocean in a fury, so that he may detect the points of real peril. He spends his time in taking soundings, climbing about on the precipitous rocks and jagged reefs, and getting drenched to the skin in the boiling surf. He is only concerned with the discovery of suitable sites for his lighthouses. They are not a pair; they are two. A pair is a single entity; its constituents are indivisible. But two are two; two separate entities, thrown together only to drift apart again. If they are a pair, all the oceans of the world may roll between them; they are united still. But if, as in the case of Abraham and Lot, Christian and Pliable, Judas and John, Stevenson and Scott, they are two, there is no union. It is mere proximity. You may bind men together by the most awful deeds and instruments that the law can devise; you may commit them to each other by the most solemn oaths and covenants; you may bring to bear upon them the most sacred rites and ceremonies; but it is all futile. They are not mated. Proximity is not affinity. They are still two; they are not a pair.

III

No one who has once experienced the torture of physical separation— the separation effected by mere distance — would say a word to belittle its inexpressible anguish. You have only to stand upon the platform when the boat-train leaves, or to take your place upon the wharf when the great ship is swinging out to sea, in order to witness one of the most poignant and passionate manifestations of human sorrow. And those who, so far from being onlookers, have actually experienced that terrible ordeal, know that it is the concentration of heartbreak and the climax of mortal agony. As the fluttering handkerchiefs become small as snowflakes and then vanish altogether; as the fond familiar faces become less and less distinguishable until at last they are lost in the crowd; as the horrid chasm slowly widens between the vessel and the quay, the soul feels itself to have been caught in the pitiless grip of heartless forces that are crushing the very life-blood out of it. At the moment it is even more painful than death. Death comes so gently and so naturally, and, for a moment or two, the dead still seem so near, that it takes a while to realize that the fond ties have been finally and irrevocably snapped. But this other wrench is so unnatural and so violent. The bitterness of death does not reach its culmination in the act and article of death. But this grief reaches its climax all in a moment; and during that moment, the soul writhes in torture indescribable. And yet, knowing this and having experienced it, I say deliberately that, of all forms of separation, this form is in reality the least intolerable.

IV

At this point Alfred Tennyson becomes our best and wisest teacher. 'In Memoriam' is the classic of two great souls whose history resembled the history of my two steamers. For a while they journeyed together and were twin. Then their ways suddenly diverged. Hallam was called to the higher service. Tennyson found himself continuing on the old course. And, contemplating the separation, the poet lets his fancy play about the various kinds of separation by which one soul may be torn from another. There is, for example, the social cleavage. Here are two ploughboys working together on the farm. They labour side by side, and are as much alike as my two steamers. But one is content to be a ploughboy; the other is fired by a great ambition. Tennyson describes this second youth as one

Who breaks his birth's invidious bar,
    And grasps the skirts of happy chance,
    And breasts the blows of circumstance,
And grapples with his evil star;

Who makes by force his merit known,
    And lives to clutch the golden keys.
    To mould a mighty state's decrees,
And shape the whisper of the throne;

And moving up from higher to higher
    Becomes, on Fortune's crowning slope,
    The pillar of a people's hope.
The centre of a world's desire.

But what about the other ploughboy, that 'earliest mate' with whom he trudged side by side along the rutted country lanes in the days of auld lang syne? He

...ploughs with pain his native lea
   And reaps the labour of his hands,
   Or in the furrow musing stands;
'Does my old friend remember me?'

Tennyson gazes upon this picture that his fancy has conjured up — the picture of the ploughman and the Prime Minister; and he compares the separation thus effected with the separation that has snatched his old friend Hallam from his side. Is Hallam like the Prime Minister, moving now along some more exalted plane? And is he himself like the ploughman, leaning on the handles of his plough, and wondering if sometimes his old friend thinks fondly of him still? Here, then, is the social cleavage. It is trying enough; but it is not the worst.

V

For, almost instantly, another picture flashes upon the white screen of the poet's fancy. A bride and bridegroom!

These two — they dwelt with eye on eye!
   Their hearts of old have beat in tune,
   Their meetings made December June,
Their every parting was to die!

Then he devotes himself to study; he must needs excel. He sits apart, lost in his researches. He seems to slight her simple heart.

He thrids the labyrinth of the mind,
   He reads the secret of the star.
   He seems so near and yet so far.
He looks so cold; she thinks him kind.

She keeps the gift of years before,
   A withered violet is her bliss;
   She knows not what his greatness is.
For that, for all, she loves him more.

For him she plays, to him she sings
   Of early faith and plighted vows;
   She knows but matters of the house.
And he, he knows a thousand things.

Her faith is fixt and cannot move,
   She darkly feels him great and wise,
   She dwells on him with faithful eyes,
'I cannot understand: I love.'

And again Tennyson thinks of his old friend. Is Hallam like the studious bridegroom? Has he lost himself in diviner contemplations and gradually-grown away from the sweet old simplicities of long ago? And is he himself like the lonely wife, gazing on her learned husband, clinging still but failing to understand?

VI

The social cleavage is bad, and the intellectual cleavage is worse, but there is something still more terrible. What about Abraham and Lot? What about Judas and John? Is not the climax of tragedy reached when two friends walk familiarly together, seek every day each other's society, and, perhaps, go up to the house of God in company.

And then; and then! One, like Abraham, becomes every day a little finer, a little nobler, a little more considerate, a little more courteous, a little more unselfish; whilst the other becomes every day a little more self-centred, a little less chivalrous, a little less thoughtful, a little more coarse, a little more materialistic, a little more sensual, until, at last, like my two steamers, no-body would ever suspect that they once journeyed so familiarly together and seemed so much alike.

Here, then, you have these five forms of human separation; these five ways in which our human partnerships may to all outward appearances be dissolved; these five methods of drifting apart.

1. There is the cleavage effected by *Distance* — the parting on the railway platform; the farewell at the wharf.

2. There is the cleavage effected by *Death* — Arthur Hallam and Alfred Tennyson.

3. There is the *Social* cleavage — the ploughboy who becomes Prime Minister, and the ploughboy who remains at his lonely furrow.

4. There is the *Intellectual* cleavage — the simple housewife and her studious husband.

5. There is the *Moral* cleavage — Abraham and Lot; John and Judas.

These five; and although I have said that, of them all, the parting on the pier is the most bitter at the moment, yet those who are called to return with swollen eyes to their saddened homes may there fall upon their knees and give humble and hearty thanks to heaven that to them has been meted out *this* form of separation — *this and no other.*

VII

Poor old Uncle Tom had been done almost to death by Simon Legree, the vicious slave-dealer. He lay in the shed, dying, his back all torn and lacerated by the cruel lashes. All through the night there stole stealthily to his side the other slaves on the plantation, poor creatures who crept in to see the last of him, to bathe his wounds, to ask his pardon, or to kneel in prayer beside his tortured frame. With the morning light came George Shelby, his old master, to redeem him.

'Is it possible, is it possible?' he exclaimed, kneeling down by the old slave. 'Uncle Tom, my poor, poor old friend!'

But Uncle Tom was too far gone. He only murmured faintly to himself:

'Jesus can make a dying bed
  Feel soft as downy pillows are.'

'You shan't die; you mustn't die, nor think of it! I've come to buy you and take you home!' cried George, with impetuous vehemence.

'Oh, Mas'r George, ye're too late. The Lord's bought me and is going to take me home — and I long to go. Heaven is better than old Kentuck!'

At this moment the sudden flush of strength which the joy of meeting his young master had infused into the dying man gave way. A sudden sinking fell upon him; he closed his eyes; and that mysterious and sublime change passed over his face that told the approach of other worlds. He began to draw his breath with long, deep inspirations; and his broad chest rose and fell heavily. The expression of his face was that of a conqueror.

'Who,' he whispered, 'who — who — who shall separate us from the love of Christ?' and fell asleep.

All the five forms of cleavage that I have tabulated had done their worst for Uncle Tom. He had been torn away from the old Kentucky home; snatched from the arms of old Aunt Chloe; sold away from children and kindred: separated from everything that he counted precious. And yet, and yet there was One heart from which nothing could separate him, One love from which he could never, never drift.

II - The Will-O'-The-Wisp

Oh, the Will-o'-the-Wisp! the Will-o'-the-Wisp I What tales we have heard of the Will-o'-the-Wisp! Hovering over the reedy mere; dancing across the misty marshes; fluttering round the dank lagoon; flickering over the spongy moorlands; who has not met with the Will-o'-the-Wisp? Child of the bog and the swamp and the fen, haunting on foggy autumn nights the soft morass and the slimy quagmire, he is known by a score of expressive and sinister *aliases*; but we are not confused by the multitude of his ugly names. Whether the country people call him Old Spunkee, or speak with terror of Jack-o'-Lantern, we recognize under each such fearsome title or description the familiar features of Will-o'-the-Wisp. How the flesh creeps as we read, in the quaint pages of Ben Jonson and Robert Burton, of John Fletcher and Francis Beaumont, their hair-raising stories of Will-o'-the-Wisp! In the first book I ever read I made the acquaintance of Will-o'-the-Wisp. It was Mary

Godolphin's *Sandford and Merton* — a special edition prepared in words of one syllable. I have it still, and a record on the fly-leaf shows that I read it first when I was in my sixth year. But I remember the tense excitement with which I followed the adventures of Hal Sandford on that night in which he was lost on the lonely moor. In front of him he saw a dim and fitful light which he took to be a lantern carried by some more fortunate traveller. The light zigzags to and fro; and Hal concludes that his fellow traveller is drunk. But, drunk or sober, he longs to reach him and enjoy some kind of human companionship. He presses on until he finds himself becoming entangled in the marshes, and at last falls headlong into a slimy pit.

'But, Hal,' says Tom Merton, as he listens to the story afterwards, 'did you find out what that light was that you saw in the marsh?'

'Yes,' said Hal; 'it was the Will-o'-the-Wisp!'

Thus, as old John Gay sings,

Will-o'-the-Wisp misleads nightfaring clowns
O'er hills and sinking bogs.

It may be with Will-o'-the-Wisp, as with most of us, that he is not so black as he is painted. It is possible that his elfish tricks have been exaggerated by those who have placed his antics and vagaries on record. Perhaps he is not so fond of damp old churchyards and places of execution as some of the novelists would have us to believe. But he is a mischievous little sprite for all that. Just listen to his song:

When night's dark mantle covers all,
I come in fire arrayed,
Many a victim I've seen fall,
Or fly from me dismayed.

Many a traveller I deceive,
And with their parting breath
I hear them call in vain for help,
And dance round them in death.

'Will-o'-the-Wisp!' they trembling cry;
'Will-o'-the-Wisp!' 'tis he!'
To mark their fright as off they fly
Is merry sport to me!

I dance! I dance! I'm here! I'm there!
Who tries to catch me catches but air!
The mortal who follows me follows in vain,
For I laugh, ha, ha!

I laugh, ho, ho!

I laugh at their folly and pain,
I laugh at their folly and pain!

II

I do not propose, in these fugitive paragraphs of mine, to attempt to reduce the subject to the terms of precise definition and exact treatment. Others have ventured upon that task, and, according to his wont, Will-o'-the-Wisp has invariably eluded them. Friedrich List, the German philosopher, came upon Will-o'-the-Wisp one night on the edge of a swamp, and held his hand in the luminous glow, yet felt no warmth. Knorr also came upon the sprite, and persuaded him to stand so still near the fringe of a marsh that he was able for a quarter of an hour to touch him by extending his walking-stick as far as he could reach over the water's edge. Yet when, at the end of that time, the light suddenly flitted away, and Knorr felt the ferrule that had been so long in the flame, it was as cold as though no fire had ever touched it. A weird, uncanny little elf is this Will-o'-the-Wisp of ours!

III

But Will-o'-the-Wisp does not stand alone. As I have wandered about the solar system, poking my stick into every ant-heap and rabbit-hole that I have come across, I have hit upon quite a number of things just as elusive and just as strange. There are lights that appear when they are most needed; lights that seem to be specially designed for the guidance of those who see them; and yet lights that will lure to his destruction the benighted creature who dares to follow them. Take Instinct, for example. Sometimes, as though to beget in us a fatal confidence in its infallibility, it leads with the most amazing accuracy along a hideously perilous and intricate path. See with what skill it guides the mason-bee! This odd little creature builds her miniature palace out of the mud. When the tiny chambers are dry and ready for occupation, she hunts for spiders. Having caught a spider, she bites him in such a way as not to kill, but to paralyse him. Then laying her eggs upon his back, she deposits him in one of the cells which she has constructed; and so on until all the cells are full. She thus secures for her offspring, in the paralysed spiders, a plentiful supply of fresh food with which to nourish their earliest infancy. Here the quality that we commonly call Instinct seems to have almost reached perfection, and it would be interesting to be able to trace the age-long history of adventure, experiment, and disappointment by which so elaborate a system has been built up and perfected. Surely the kindly light that leads the mason-bee so shrewdly can be safely trusted by everything and everybody!

And yet, and yet! Travellers on the Amazon have frequently commented upon the fate that overtakes vast numbers of boa-constrictors when the river is swollen with its winter floods. Instinct teaches these huge reptiles, in the autumn, to take a full meal and coil themselves up for their long sleep. But, strangely enough. Instinct does not teach them where to hibernate. As a consequence, great numbers of them coil themselves up *below high-water-mark*, with the result that, when the rains come and the river rises, they are swept away by the swirling waters. Instinct tells them *what* to do and *when* to do it; but it does not tell them *where* to do it, and for the want of this essential item of information they miserably perish. Or pass from the insects and the reptiles to the animals. Let us take the case of the lemmings. 'Every now and then,' says a traveller who has seen this strange phenomenon in Norway, 'every now and then, all the lemmings in a district congregate in a great army, as if some Fiery Cross summons has been sent round, and move in a bee-line for the sea. Over mountains, through forests, across foaming torrents they make their impetuous way. Many are lost, many drop, many starve; but on and on the army marches for the sea. And when they reach the sea, all plunge in *and are drowned!* What perverted instinct can account for this?' In this case it would almost seem as if Instinct had not merely forgotten, as in the case of the boa-constrictor, to tell the creatures something that they need to know, but had deliberately set herself to lure them to their doom. Is not this a Will-o'-the-Wisp?

One of the novelists to whom I have referred tells of a peculiarly grim adventure. His hero, hopelessly lost in a lonely and unfamiliar district, sees all at once two lights. One, a long way off, appears to be passing through a clump of trees. Its bearer is apparently on the fringe of a forest. The traveller shrinks from the thought of entering the gloomy woods at dead of night, and turns wistfully towards the other gleam. It is nearer; it advances slowly, though with irregular and jaunty movements, across the level country. He decides to follow it, and is soon up to his waist in the swamp. As it turned out, the distant light was the lantern of the men who were searching for him; he had been ensnared by the glow of the Will-o'-the Wisp! Now something very like this is happening every day. There are well-known cases of conflicting instincts, or of an instinct that speaks simultaneously with two contradictory voices. Darwin, in his *Descent of Man,* gives several instances of this peculiarity. The most curious, in his judgment, is the occasional conquest of the maternal instinct by the migratory instinct. The *maternal* instinct is one of the most powerful emotions known to naturalists. It will lead the most feeble, the most timid, and the most shrinking creatures to face the greatest dangers in direct opposition to the law of self-preservation. But the *migratory* instinct is also amazingly strong. 'A confined bird will at the proper season beat her breast against the wires of her cage until it is bare and bloody. The migratory instinct causes young salmon to leap out of fresh water, in which they could continue to exist, and thus unintentionally to commit suicide.' And it sometimes happens that these two instincts, the maternal and the migratory, appeal to the same bird at the same time. Thus, late in the autumn, swallows, house-martins, and swifts frequently desert the tender young in their nests. Darwin thought that, when the bird is near her nestlings, the *maternal* instinct is probably the stronger; but when, out of sight of the nest, she comes upon thousands of other swallows congregating for their overseas flight, the *migratory* instinct assumes the ascendant. 'When arrived at the end of her long journey, and the migratory instinct has ceased to act, what an agony of remorse the bird must feel, if, from being endowed with great mental activity, she cannot prevent the image constantly passing before her mind of her young ones perishing through cold and hunger on a bleak and distant shore!' Is not this the very experience that the novelist describes?

IV

Is Reason much better — or even Conscience? Reason is a most marvellous faculty. And yet, in the straits of the soul, it is a most erratic guide. Two statesmen, equally able and equally conscientious, survey the same facts; reach diametrically opposite conclusions; and become the leaders of hostile parties. Two scientists, equally discerning and equally experienced, examine the same phenomena, and build up theories utterly antagonistic the one to the other. Two judges, equally learned and equally just, hear the same witnesses tell the same stories; they convince the one judge that truth is with the prosecutor, whilst the other is no less certain that it is with the defendant. If I trust so treacherous a guide too implicitly, may I not find myself floundering in the bog?

Conscience, too, is wonderful, almost divine. And yet, as has often been pointed out, 'when the Lacedaemonians whipped boys to death as an offering to Diana; when the mother of Xerxes, as he departed on one of his expeditions, buried alive a number of youths to propitiate the subterranean powers; when the Carthaginians placed their little children on the red-hot lap of Moloch,' they were following Conscience and making terrible sacrifices for her dear sake. The men who burned the martyrs were often as conscientious as the martyrs whom they burned. When, on the first of July, 1416, John Huss was bound to the stake, a poor old peasant woman came to the place of execution bringing with her a faggot. She begged that it might be added to the pile round the stake. But when it was flung on, she was not content. It must, she said, be close up to the victim, so that it might help to consume him.

'Have I ever harmed you or yours,' asked Huss, 'that you are so bitter against me?'

'Never,' was the reply; 'but you are a heretic. Wood is scarce this year, and the winter, they say, is like to be a hard one. I can ill afford the faggot, but I would fain do God service by helping to rid the earth of an accursed heretic; and therefore I make the sacrifice.'

'O holy simplicity!' exclaimed the martyr. And, reaching out his hand, he drew the faggot toward him, and placed it against his side. 'Perhaps,' he said, 'the faggot may be a means of grace to both of us!'

'Give your body to be burned!' said Conscience to John Huss. 'Give your faggot to burn him!' said Conscience to the peasant woman.

Is not this the Will-o'-the-Wisp?

V

Then spake Jesus unto them, saying: 'I am the Light of the World: he that followeth Me shall not walk in darkness, but shall have THE Light of Life.' And with that golden word of clear guidance ringing in our ears we say goodbye for ever to the Will-o'-the-Wisp.

III - The Doctor's Conversion

I WISH I could introduce the old doctor in some more human fashion. Pen and ink are all very well in their way, but their way is not the best way. And no way but the best way is worthy of the doctor. You need to see him, to hear his voice, to feel his handclasp, and to breathe the atmosphere that is generated by his presence. I can never hope, through this lame medium, to give any impression of his bulky, though not ungainly, form; his venerable countenance; his silvery hair; his sparkling eyes; his deep, rich, musical voice. It is worth a mile's walk on a wet day just to hear him laugh. An evening with the doctor is one of the luxuries of life.

As everybody knows. Doctor John Horner is the beloved and honoured minister of the church at Willoughby Street. He lives in the old stone, ivy-covered house behind the church, and the gloomy walk under the chestnut-trees to his door has been well worn by a constant stream of eager visitors. Young people have walked along this shady path at the very summit of their felicity; and older folk have sometimes carried along it hearts as heavy as lead. For the doctor has been here now for over thirty years. He has watched the members of the Willoughby Street congregation grow up from childhood. Mr. Edward Westbrook, the secretary of the church, and his wife, are both of them conscious of silver in their hair. But the doctor likes to remind them of a certain Sunday, in the early days of their courtship, when they sat together in church for the first time. The doctor has shared with them all the joys and sorrows of their happy wedded life. When each of the children was but a few days old, he stood reverently by the bedside and breathed upon mother and babe his benediction. When, fifteen years ago, Lily, the only daughter, a fair but frail girl, drooped and died, he, by his very presence, radiated comfort and courage in the stricken home. When business affairs are not going just to Mr. Westbrook's liking, he always says that a chat with the doctor is as bracing as a tonic or a holiday. 'I always go back to the office whistling next morning,' he says, when he tells you about it. And when things at home are causing headache or heartache, it is to the doctor that Mrs. Westbrook always carries her worries. 'Somehow or other,' she says, 'he always seems to understand. He listens to all that I say, and talks it over with me afterwards just as if the affairs we are discussing were his own. I have often seen his eyes moisten when we have been in trouble. But by the time that he has talked with me and prayed with me, I always feel that the worst is over, and that everything will be sure to come right after all.' Any of the scores of men and women whom you may see sitting with their young people in the stately old pews at Willoughby Street would speak of the doctor in exactly the same way. It is always a congenial topic of conversation. In every allusion that they make to him there is a singular mingling of reverence and endearment. The doctor has made himself the father of all his people; and, in the process, he has converted his pulpit into a throne.

II

For years after I met first the doctor I took it for granted that he had always been of the temper that we all so greatly honoured and so much admired. But one evening I made a discovery that quite astounded me. I had undertaken to preach some special sermons at Whitlington, and was met at the railway station by the minister of the church. After a cheerful tea and a short stroll, we settled down to an evening by the fireside. My hostess and her daughter busied themselves with their knitting; the minister and I just talked. I learned with surprise that he and the doctor were at college together. Instantly the current of our conversation set steadily along that channel. The theme was of mutual interest, and seemed almost inexhaustible. All at once I made my discovery.

'Yes,' remarked my host, leaning back in his chair meditatively, 'I have never seen a greater change overtake the minister than the change that came over John Horner after he went to Willoughby Street.'

'Indeed,' I replied, 'and in what way?'

'Oh, when next you see him, you must ask him to tell you the story of his conversion, as he calls it. As I told you, we were in college together; and we settled at about the same time in towns not far apart — he at Oakhampton and I at Trowford. John was eight years at Oakhampton before he was called to Willoughby Street; and he was in hot water all the time!'

'In hot water!' I exclaimed in astonishment.

'In those days,' my host continued, 'John Horner was the greatest controversialist in our part of the country. He was always pitching into somebody. Once or twice a week, when you picked up the paper, you could rely upon finding a letter signed "John Horner" protesting against some local proposal or exposing the fallacy of somebody's argument. In almost every sermon he launched some violent attack or brought some scathing indictment. In such wordy warfare he was a most skilful swordsman. He knew how to thrust and how to parry. He was continually debating, contending, disputing; he was never happy unless some fierce storm of controversy was raging around him. Whenever he came to see me, he would rub his hands and ask, with eyes sparkling, and all his body in a ferment of excitement, whether I had seen his letter in the *Courier.* "I've left him," he would exclaim, "without a leg to stand on; he'll never dare to reply!" To the religious papers, also, John sent his terrible philippics. He was the heart and soul of many a heated disputation; people knew, as soon as they saw his signature at the foot of a communication, that things were likely to be lively; and editors welcomed his contributions for the sake of the simmer of excitement that they imparted to columns that were too often unconscionably dull. John gloried in a fight. I told him once that he reminded me of George Macdonald's "Waesome Carl."

There cam a man to oor toon-en',
And a waesome carl was he,
· · · · · · ·
Muckle he spied, and muckle he spak,
But the owercome o' his sang,
Whatever it said, was aye the same: —

There's nane o' ye but's a' wrangl
Ye're a' wrang, and a' wrang.
And a'thegither a' wrang;
There's no a man aboot the toon
But's a'thegither a' wrang.

As soon as the words were out of my mouth, I could see that John resented them. But he was on his defence in a moment. His eyes flashed. True religion, he exclaimed, is virile, militant, aggressive. The whole spirit of apostolic evangelism, he maintained, was in the nature of a tremendous and sustained contention. Most of us, he declared, are too mealy-mouthed. Then, warming to his subject, he crushed me beneath a perfect avalanche of argument. He overwhelmed me with an impressive pageant of ponderous authorities. I cowered before the fusillade and cannonade to which he pitilessly subjected me. Most heartily did I regret having had the temerity, on even a minor point, to differ from him. In those days John kept the whole town in a ferment. But you must ask him, when you go back, to tell you all about it. Say I told you to.'

III

The opportunity came more quickly than I could have expected. A few days later I was strolling through the park. I crossed the lawns and made my way down to the lake; and standing at the water's edge, watching the children feeding the swans, I saw the doctor himself. He greeted me warmly, and led me to a seat under a giant elm, and we sat there enjoying the glorious expanse of green grass, noble forestry, and shimmering water that, like a panorama, spread itself out before us. My opportunity was not long in coming. He asked me about my visit to Whitlington. Had I seen his old friend there? And how were things going with him? I told him of the services, of the affairs of the Whitlington household, and then of the talk beside the fire. As soon as I had mentioned it, I saw that I had unwittingly revived an unpleasant memory. A cloud passed over his face, and he sat in silence, apparently looking at the swans. Then, all at once, he broke into laughter — laughter that had a little undertone of sadness — and began.

'Ah, well,' he exclaimed, 'an old minister ought not to be above telling a young minister of his early blunders; and that was certainly one of mine. At Oakhampton I indulged pretty freely my insatiable fondness for controversy, and I suppose I was fairly clever at it. But it was a mistake for all that. It doesn't pay, my dear fellow, it doesn't pay. I call those my "Jack Horner" days.' He laughed again, more heartily this time. 'I don't suppose,' he went on, 'I don't suppose the nursery rhyme was intended as a personal attack upon myself, although it takes liberties with my name; but it describes me to a nicety. I was everlastingly putting in my thumb and pulling out a plum and saying "What a good boy am I!" I spent seven years in this way; and then a thing happened that set me thinking. I was summoned one evening to visit a man who was dying. He was not a member of my own congregation; but his minister was out of town, and he expressed a desire to see me. I went to him; reminded him of the immutable foundations of our everlasting hope; prayed with him; and was coming away filled with those emotions which every minister experiences under such conditions. As I gently clasped the dying man's hand to take farewell, he looked into my face with a strange and wistful sadness, and observed:

"'I wish I had understood you better years ago!"

"'Indeed!" I exclaimed. "And in what way?"

'And then he told me that it was by means of my ministry that he had been led into the kingdom and service of Jesus Christ. He had come to the church one evening; I had preached a fervent evangelistic sermon; his attention was riveted, his soul was stirred, he had found his way to the Saviour.

"'I came back the following Sunday," he went on to say, "but you were engaged in attacking the proposals of the Public Buildings Committee; and the following Sunday you were exploding the arguments of a certain Mr. Clinton. All that you said was very good and very true, and it was said with moderation and with judgment; but, somehow, I felt that I could not nourish my newly found faith on that kind of thing; so I went the following Sunday to St. John's, and eventually joined that congregation. But as I listened just now to all that you said, and followed you in prayer, I could not help feeling what a gain it would have been to me had I understood you more perfectly."'

The doctor rose from my side and strolled a few feet in the direction of the lake, pretending to be interested in some of the elm leaves which he picked up, autumn leaves that had come fluttering down whilst he told me his story. He tossed the leaves away again, and resumed his seat.

'He did not mean it as a rebuke,' he went on. 'He merely intended it as a kind acknowledgment of my services and as a personal regret. But coming from the lips of a dying man, it affected me more than anything I had heard for years. This all happened on the Tuesday. On the Friday I buried him; and during those days I could think about nothing else.'

He paused, and again seemed to be watching the swans, which, by this time, were out among the water-lilies in the centre of the lake.

'During those days,' he continued, 'everything that I read and everything that I heard seemed to bear in some strange way upon that bedside conversation. It mattered little what book I took down from my shelves — theology, history, science, fiction — it was all the same. It seemed bent upon rebuking my contentious spirit. You know how, when one dominating idea holds all your mind, everything that you see and hear seems to stand related to it. So was it with me. I was reading at the time an old classic by Isaac Barrow, Newton's famous preceptor. I had scarcely opened the book that morning before the old professor began on this very theme. "Avoid controversy at any cost," he says. "The truth contended for is not worth the passion expended upon it. The benefits of the victory do not atone for the prejudices aroused in the combat. Goodness and virtue may often consist with ignorance and error, seldom with strife and discord." With a heavy heart, I laid the volume aside; and took down Richard Baxter, who first taught me how to be a minister. But — would you believe it? — I had not got through half a dozen pages before my old master burst out upon me. "Another fatal hindrance," he said, "to a heavenly walk and conversation is our too frequent disputes. A disputatious spirit is a sure sign of an unsanctified spirit. They are usually men least acquainted with the heavenly life who are the most violent disputers about the circumstantiality of religion. Yea, though you were sure that your opinions were true, yet when the chiefest of your zeal is turned to these things, the life of grace soon decays within. The least controverted truths are usually the most weighty and of most necessary and frequent use to our souls." I felt that my old master had but rubbed brine into my smarting wounds, and I returned him sadly to the shelf. That very afternoon I had occasion to dip into John Wesley's *Journal,* and under date October 9, 1741, I stumbled upon this: "I found Mr. Humphreys with Mr. Simpson. They immediately fell upon their favourite subject; on which, when we had disputed two hours, and were just where we were at first, I begged we might exchange controversy for prayer. We did so, and then parted in much love, about two in the morning." In sheer despair I returned Wesley to his place, and forsook the theologians altogether. I picked up a volume of Darwin which, newly purchased, lay uncut on the desk. But, to my amazement, he was harping on the same old theme. "I rejoice," he said, "that I have avoided controversies, and this I owe to Lyell, who many years ago, in reference to my geological works, strongly advised me never to get entangled in a controversy, as it rarely did any good, and caused a miserable loss of time and temper." I put the volume back on the desk; and, fancying that relief would surely come with fiction, I slipped a novel into my pocket and, after tea, went out into the fields. It happened to be Mark Rutherford's *Revolution in Tanner's Lane.* Imagine my consternation on finding one of the characters, Zachariah Coleman, talking on this very subject! No controversy can be of any use, he says. "It leads to everlasting debate, and it is not genuine debate, for nobody really ranges himself alongside his enemy's strongest points! It encourages all sorts of sophistry, becomes mere manoeuvring, and saps people's faith in the truth." I went back to the house. How I spent the rest of the evening does not matter much to you or anybody else; but from that day to this I have never entangled myself in controversy again.'

It was getting chilly; the dusk was falling, and we could no longer see the swans. We rose from the seat under the elm, and I saw the doctor to his home. As I walked back along the path under the chestnut trees, I thought of all that Mr. Westbrook and others had told me of the doctor's long, rich, fruitful ministry at Willoughby Street; and I felt that the vow that he registered on that memorable night, more than thirty years ago, had been well kept and amply vindicated.

IV - Heather and Bluebells

Come with me, and I will show you a few things well worth seeing, and introduce you to a few folk well worth meeting! And I promise that you will not look back upon our excursion as time thrown away! Come along!

I

And first to Scotland! All ministers have a soft place in their hearts for Scotland, and with good reason. Ministers, as becomes men who long to excel, glory in reading the noble records of those historic ministries that will stand as a model to all ministers as long as time shall last. And of such classical ministries Scotland has had more than its share. And no wonder! Every clearcut phase of national existence has its own ideal. The life of Greece, essentially contemplative, found its ideal in the *Philosopher*. The life of Rome, essentially militant, found its ideal in the *Soldier*. The life of Judea, essentially religious, found its ideal in the *Prophet*. But just once in the world's chequered history, one little nation, during a brief but memorable epoch in its story, found its ideal in the *Minister*. Every Scottish father looked into the face of his boy and felt that it would be life's crowning honour, a consummation worthy of any sacrifice, if that boy of his were to be called to the sacred engagements of the Christian ministry.

The old schoolmaster of Drumtochty, everywhere beloved and everywhere revered, did not often visit the homes of his pupils. But when he did, all the Glen knew that something of unusual importance was afoot.

'George is a fine laddie, Mrs. Howe,' he said on one of those rare occasions. 'What do you think of making him?'

Marget knew that the great hour of her life had come, the hour for which she had longed and wept and prayed. 'There was just a single ambition in those humble homes,' says Ian Maclaren, 'the ambition to have one member of the family at college; and if Domsie approved a lad, then his brothers and sisters would give their wages and the family would live on skim milk and oatcake to let him have his chance.'

'Maister Jamieson,' said Marget, 'ma hert's desire is to see George a minister; and if the Almighty spared me to hear ma only bairn open his mooth in the Evangel, I would hae naething mair to ask...but I doot sair it canna be managed!'

Out of so warm and congenial an atmosphere there arose, as was to be expected, great ministers and great ministries. Now, standing on this bleak and windswept hilltop, the heather almost up to your knees, the shining waters of Loch Leven on the one hand and the deep glades of Dunsinane Wood on the other, have a good look around you! For here, among these hills and valleys, there lived, not so very long ago, a group of ministers whose fragrant influence will abide upon this dusty old world of ours to its very latest day. To dip into any one of their biographies is like stepping into a garden of roses. For here, within easy riding distance of each other, there lived and laboured Robert Murray McCheyne, W. C. Burns, Alexander Somerville, Andrew and Horatius Bonar, and a number of other kindred spirits whose names are scarcely less familiar. They all dwelt hereabouts. But come, the wind is too keen upon the hilltop; let us stretch our legs! We will stroll down through the wood, in which primroses are twinkling and the squirrels making merry, into the odd little village of Kinrossie. Passing its pretty thatched cottages, its sleepy village green, and its quaint old market-cross, we will continue our stroll until we come suddenly upon the Free Kirk of Collace. It was here that Andrew Bonar — after whom Mr. Bonar Law is named — ministered for many years. Not far away, just on the fringe of the wood, is the old manse, almost hidden by its tall hedges and its clump of gloomy trees. You must come inside. This was Andrew Bonar's study. It is a dreamy old room, with a vine and a fig-tree climbing up on either side of one of the windows. Now turn from that window to this one, and look not *through* it but *over* it. And carved deeply into the oak above the window you will see three Hebrew words. Translate them, and you have a text from the Book of Proverbs. *'He that winneth souls is wise.'* We are in no mood to-day to plunge into the grime and smoke of cities; but take my word for it that if we went to Glasgow, and visited the church in which Dr. Bonar exercised his later ministry, you would find the same three Hebrew words carved into the pulpit desk. Standing in this quiet room, looking out on to this beautiful countryside, this Hebrew inscription seems strangely to revive the spirit and temper of that handful of devoted and scholarly and faithful ministers who, less than a century ago, made these heathery hills and primrosed valleys to ring with the name and fame of their Lord.

To England now! And again we will keep far from the cities with their dust and smoke. Walk with me down this winding old lane, with its great elms arching overhead and its hedgerows all ablaze with hyacinths, stitchworts, vetches, and wild strawberries, and we shall come to a laughing little stream. You can trace its course, even at this distance, by the willows along its banks. The rabbits, startled by our approach, scurry into their burrows under the hedge; a hare goes bounding off along the lane; and the finches are busy in the hawthorn. But here is a stile! We will take this short cut across the fields to the waterside. Just look at the bluebells and the daffodils waving on both banks! A water-rat, uncertain as to our intentions, decides to take no risks. He drops with a splash into the water and strikes out bravely for the opposite shore. We saunter gently along the side of the stream for half an hour, soothed by the music of its murmur, and then we discover that this tranquil paradise is no monopoly of ours. There, just round the bend of the stream, sits a gentle old man, with rod in hand, his basket beside him, and his attention riveted upon his line. Now, to tell the whole truth, it is to meet this good old English gentleman that I have brought you here. He is one of the most lovable, one of the most thoughtful, and in every way one of the best men of his time. His hair is white as snow; there is a slight stoop at the shoulders, partly caused by age and partly by much bending over his beloved reel; but these are the only hints he gives of having long since passed his eightieth birthday. His face is strong and sometimes sad — for he has known terrible sorrows — yet it is suffused by a certain indescribable sweetness. His eye is bright and keen, especially when near the water, yet always infinitely restful. He is dressed neither showily nor shabbily, but with a pleasant trimness that suggests dignity and self-respect. When we speak to him you will discover that his voice is as soft as velvet and as musical as the waters beside which he spends his days. No Englishman is better worth knowing. He breathes, as Lamb said to Coleridge, the very spirit of innocence, purity, and simplicity of heart. For this is Izaak Walton, courtly, scholarly, saintly; and I have reasons of my own for seeking his society to-day.

As soon as I discovered the three Hebrew words over Andrew Bonar's window in the old manse at Kinrossie, and again on the pulpit desk at Glasgow, I turned at once to the commentators. The words had aroused my curiosity, and I was anxious to ascertain their exact significance. *'He that winneth souls is wise.'* The commentators, however, disappointed me. They suggested that the verb translated 'winneth' is an angler's word; and then, like battleships hard pressed, they vanished in a cloud of smoke. Still, in a world like this, we must be thankful for small mercies; and the commentators have at least given us an interesting clue. He that is wise catcheth souls as an angler catches fish. Now if there is one man among my circle of friends who knows everything about angling it is old Izaak Walton. To him, therefore, always the soul of patience with honest inquirers, let us submit our problem. We must state it in the abstract. It is of no use mentioning the manse at Kinrossie, or the church at Glasgow; for Andrew Bonar was not born until poor old Izaak's bones had rested for more than a hundred years in their peaceful and grassy grave. To you and me, sublimely superior to the trivial accidents of time and space, that is a mere circumstance; but the old gentleman himself might find it a little confusing. The three Hebrew words, however, stood upon the pages of his Bible just as they stood upon the pages of Andrew Bonar's Bible; and just as they stand upon the pages of mine. See! The old gentleman has risen; he has thrown some ground-bait into the stream to secure his sport for the afternoon; and now he is retiring for the enjoyment of his lunch to a cosy niche against the gnarled trunk of that old willowtree! Let us go forward!

III

'The words bear out,' says the gentle old man, after we have duly introduced ourselves and explained our mission, 'the words bear out what I have so often said to my own honest scholars. The work of catching men is very similar to the sport of catching fish. That is why four anglers — Peter, Andrew, James, and John — had priority of nomination in the catalogue of the twelve apostles. Our Saviour found that the hearts of such men were, by nature, fitted for contemplation and quietness; they were men of mild and sweet and peaceable spirits, as most anglers are. The words that have puzzled you mean that to be a successful fisherman, a man must be very fond of his work. He must love fishing and give his whole mind to it. Master John Bunyan, in that strange conceit which he has this very year published and which he calls his Pilgrim's Progress, truly says:

> You see the way the fisherman doth take
> To catch the fish; what engines doth he make!
> Behold how he engageth all his wits;
> Also his snares, lines, angles, hooks, and nets:
>
> Yet fish there be that neither hook nor line,
> Nor snare, nor net, nor engine can make thine;
> They must be groped for and be tickled too,
> Or they will not be catch'd, whate'er you do.

'Now in order that you may the better perceive the meaning of these three Hebrew words that have so perplexed you, let me teach you the four rules of the angler's art, which I have cast into verse that they may be the more readily retained in the recollection of my own scholars:

> Be sure your face is towards the light:
>   Study the fish's curious ways:
> Then keep yourself well out of sight:
>   And cherish Patience all your days.

He that will learn those four precepts and obey them will make a happy and successful angler, and will, if he so desire, acquire the wisdom that is celebrated in the Hebrew words you brought me.' By this time the old gentleman has finished his lunch and is looking wistfully towards the spot that he so well stocked with ground-bait. We may wish him a merry afternoon's sport and take our leave of him.

IV

And now, before we ourselves part company, let us spend a moment in my study surveying the spoils of our expedition. We have the three Hebrew words that we brought back from Scotland — *'He that winneth souls is wise.'* And we have this curious specimen of versification that we picked up among the bluebells by the English stream:

Be sure your face is towards the light:
    Study the fish's curious ways:
Then keep yourself well out of sight:
    And cherish Patience all your days.

What are we to make of this? Let us take it to pieces, and examine the various parts under a microscope. And let the Angels of the Four Corners of My Study unfold its hidden meanings to us.

'Be sure your face is towards the light!' 'The skilful angler will always be careful to see,' says the Angel of the Eastern Corner, 'that the sun shines upon his face and that his shadow falls behind him. He who turns his back to the sun and lets his shadow darken the stream has said good-bye to all the trout. The only man who can hopefully angle for fish or for folk is he of the Radiant Face, he of the Shadow Unseen!'

'Study the fish's curious ways!' 'Let no man think,' exclaims the Angel of the Western Corner, 'that he can become a successful angler by learning all about lines and hooks and rods and reels! He must study *fish.* He must mark their varying habits, watch their curious ways, and consider their fastidious tastes. He must know the things that please them, the things that repel them, and the places in which they love to lie. He who would catch *fish* must study *fish;* he who would catch *men* must understand *men!'*

'Then keep yourself well out of sight!' 'He who would return from the riverbank with a heavy basket,' observes the Angel of the North Corner, 'must angle with a long line! He must keep as far from the stream as he possibly can. No man ever yet secured large catches, either of fish or of men, who was fond of thrusting himself into inordinate prominence!'

'And cherish Patience all your days!' 'You will need it,' exclaims the Angel of the South Corner. 'There will be times when you will have to wait for long, long periods without so much as a nibble; and you will be tempted to give it all up! And you will be beset by a multitude of unexpected difficulties. "Oh,

the tangles, more than Gordian, of gut on a windy day! Oh, bitter east wind that bloweth down stream! Oh, the young ducks that, swimming between us and the trout, contend with him for the blue duns in their season! Oh, the hay grass behind us that entangles the hook! Oh, the rocky wall that breaks it, the boughs that catch it; the drought that leaves the salmon-stream dry, the floods that fill it with turbid, impassable waters! Alas, for the knot that breaks, and for the iron that bends; for the lost landing-net and the gillie that scrapes the fish!" But the angler who has the spirit of his craft will keep smiling in spite of long delays and heart-breaking disappointments, and will enjoy the unspeakable rapture of the fisherman's triumph at the last!'

V

And somehow I fancy that the Angels of the Four Corners have unwittingly expounded for us, not only the quaint old jingle that we found among the English bluebells, but those majestic Hebrew words that we saw amidst the Scottish heather.

V - The Village Green

A WISE old place is the Village Green. Since last I felt upon my spirit the fragrant breath of its peaceful benediction, I have crossed many seas and trodden many shores, but nowhere have I seen anything to equal it. Like all the best things in life, the Green is very modest; it does not advertise its virtues. As you drive round the bend of the dusty road, and, before plunging into the village itself, glance casually across the Green, you feel that it is the very essence of idyllic stagnation and dreamy repose. The signs of life are few and far between. Two old men sit smoking their long clay pipes in the deep shade of the clump of elm-trees in front of the inn; some ducks are scouring the pond yonder in quest of the frogs whose hoarse voices were so conspicuous last night; half a dozen cows lie, sleepily chewing the cud, round on the far fringe of the Green, where the grass is long and sweet, because scarcely ever trodden; some fowls from the row of cottages at the corner of the lane are foraging after grasshoppers in the shorter grass down by the poplars; swallows are skimming gracefully hither and thither, paying frequent visits to the pond, and occasionally settling for just a moment on rails and posts and empty seats; a few creamy butterflies are dancing gaily over the grass on their way to the flaunting sunflowers that call loudly from the garden of the inn; but, save for these, there are no indications that anything is doing on the Green. To all intents and purposes the Green is fast asleep, and everything about it is also slumbering in the luxurious sunshine of this summer afternoon.

Look across the pond, and you will see the old church sleeping among its gnarled and shady yews. The inn, down by the elms, is asleep. The horses round about the door, and the dogs sprawling at their feet, are all asleep. The cottages down at the corner of the lane are dozing too; lulled to rest by the droning of the bees around their scent-laden gardens. Everything appears to slumber. The very grasses nod half sleepily, and the whole place is wrapped in profound repose. You jump to the conclusion that nothing ever happens on the Village Green. But that is part of life's vast illusion. The people who do the world's work are all of them leisurely souls; they never hustle or bustle; they never get flurried or flushed.

I once attended a farewell meeting tendered to a minister who, after a remarkably fruitful and prosperous pastorate extending over more than twenty years, was laying down his charge. The great hall was crowded; there was a sense of genuine sadness and poignant emotion in the temper of the meeting; the speakers vied with each other in sounding the good man's praises. I have forgotten all that they said. But I distinctly remember the utterance of a man who, towards the close of the meeting, craved the chairman's permission to add a single sentence. 'I have met Mr. Falkland nearly every day of my life for twenty years,' he said, 'and I have never yet seen him in a hurry!' Mr. Falkland told me afterwards that he treasured that tribute as the highest of the compliments paid him at the meeting. He had entered into the secret of the Village Green.

There are souls that are so calm just because they are so strong. Mr. Harold Begbie has told us the story of Dolly, the actress, who, amidst all the whirl and the excitement of her public life, was overtaken by an affliction that rendered her stone deaf. Then, at last, freed from the rush and flurry of things, she had time to think. She thought especially of her children. Would she like them to model their lives on the style of her own? Then she thought of her widowed mother-in-law, so quiet, so tranquil, so patient, yet so strong. As she contemplated the life and character of this beautiful old lady, Dolly felt for the first time the wisdom of goodness. 'She had lived a good life; her heart was pure; her hands were clean; her eyes were full of sweetness.' But she was dying. Dolly determined to hasten to her bedside and crave of her, so that she might hand it on to her children, the inner secret of her radiant and lovely life.

'The widow put out her hand towards her Bible, but checked herself, and took a pencil and tablet which rested on a table at her side, and wrote the words:

In returning and rest shall ye be saved;
In quietness and in confidence shall be your strength.

She did not point out the words in Isaiah, because, with her fine spirit, her thoughtfulness for others, which lasted to the very end of her life, she knew that poor Dolly would be hurt by the concluding words, *"And ye would not."*

Her finger pointed to the word "Rest" for a long time. Then it moved to *"Quietness,"* and *"Confidence,"* and finally to *"Strength,"* where it tarried. Then she gave the paper to Dolly, and smiled into her eyes.' The strength of stillness! The conquest of the quiet! That is the secret of the Village Green.

You would think, I say, to look at the Village Green, that nothing ever happens there. The fact is, of course, that everything happens there. The Village Green is a parliament and a playground and a pasture and a pulpit — and everything else! Why, on the old seats there under the elm-trees, the seats that are smothered with rudely carved initials, the village cronies have sat smoking in the dusk, generation after generation, discussing the merits of rival statesmen and the splendid problems of empire. Out there, too, on the centre of the Green, cricket-matches have been played that have, for long weeks beforehand, been the subject of animated speculation among all the hamlets and villages for miles around; and that have, in the result, made history. For you would not dare to confess, to the enthusiasts who sometimes gather beneath the elms, or sprawl upon the soft and fragrant grass, that you have never witnessed the prowess of certain well-known players who, once the pride of this very Green, were elevated to the fierce prominence of county contests, and are now named with respect in every pavilion and clubroom throughout the world! On any Saturday afternoon, or in the long delicious evenings of midsummer, you may stand here on the edge of the Green, and, whilst the swallows skim cunningly about you, may hear these ploughmen and wagoners, bent with the heavy toils of tilth and pasture, tell for the thousandth time of the wild excitements that convulsed the Green in their days when a batsman of undying fame, who afterwards achieved international distinction, was the terror of every visiting team.

Nor must I forget the avenue. Running right athwart the Green — leaving the cricket-ground, the clump of elms, and the inn on the one side; and the pond, the poplars, and the drowsy old church on the other — is a glorious grove of stately oaks. Here again, every fifty yards or so, you will find seats beneath the trees. But you will notice that, in contrast with those under the elms, *these* seats are almost innocent of the carved initials. It is true that these are not quite as ancient as those; but that, in itself, does not explain the difference. When these seats have held their places as long as those beneath the elms have now done, the number of initials cut in the wood will still be very small. The reason is not very obscure. The elm-trees, with the seats beneath them, form a natural pavilion for the cricket-matches and the sports upon the Green. There schoolboys congregate, having in their cavernous and comprehensive pockets knives of such superior calibre and keenness that 'twere a pity not sometimes to display their powers! And generations of batsmen, waiting, during the innings of their side, for their own turn to bat — or to field — have relieved the hours of tedium by plying their nervous fingers there. But the avenue is never the resort of the crowd. The avenue, you would soon learn if you stayed many days in the village, is consecrated by long tradition to the sacred rites and ancient mysteries of love-making. You cannot stroll up this umbrageous roadway after dusk without meeting at least one couple who will make you feel that they can content themselves without your company. And you will discover, perhaps with some slight flush of embarrassment, that all the seats are not unoccupied. It is just as well that these wooden things are mute. If they became magically invested with the power of speech, every housewife in the village would clamour for their destruction, for have they not heard the whispered secrets of every home? The lovers of six generations have trysted and courted and quarrelled — and kissed again — within the shady shelter of these protecting trees; and they may have had reasons of their own for not carving their names upon the seats. Perhaps the light was not too good; perhaps they had other fish to fry; perhaps they had no desire to leave a perpetual record of their presence there. At any rate, the seats beneath the oaks escape such mutilation, as any one can see who cares to look.

Grave and gay is the Village Green. If you want to see its gaiety, come some winter's day when the pond is frozen, and half the countryside is on skates. Or, better still, come some winter's night. I remember walking down to the Green one delectable moonlight evening, when everything was sparkling with the glittering whiteness of the heavy hoar frost. The arched network of branches overhead looked as though it had been worked in silver and sprinkled with star-dust. It was bespangled with millions of infinitesimal diamonds. Showers of these tiny gems seemed to have fallen off, bejewelling the road beneath. It glistened in front of you, and clanked like iron beneath your tread. How one's cheeks glowed and one's ears tingled on a radiant night like that! And long before I reached the Green I could hear the shouts and laughter of the skaters on the pond. Or, if you are not prepared to wait for such another winter's day, come along some fine morning when the hounds meet at the inn! The bravery of the huntsmen, resplendent in their scarlet coats; the pride of the glossy horses, all restless with life and eager to be off; the joviality and excitement of their masters and mistresses, some in the saddle and some standing in little groups holding their horses' heads; the yelping of the dogs; the sounding of the horn; the chatter of the cottagers who have come to see the start — here is gaiety such as none of your crowded cities could give you on an autumn morning! Or, if you would see the Green taking its nighttime merriment, come on the evening of a fair-day or a fete-day, when the trees all twinkle with fairy-lamps; the village band plays near the elm-trees; and there is dancing on the Green. The trampling on the grass of so many feet loads the evening air with the strong, pungent odour of the turf; the mind is intoxicated with the prevailing sense of revelry; and the muscles dance involuntarily to the lively and captivating strains.

Oh, yes, the Green knows how to be gay; but the Green knows how to be grave. Have I not seen the Village Green turned into a church, and that not once, but many a time? As a boy I heard Mr. Moody preaching on the Village Green. He was the first preacher of world-wide fame to whom I had ever listened. I have heard many of our pulpit princes since; and often, in the years that followed that service on the Green, I again heard Mr. Moody. But, when I think of him, it is the thought of that Sunday afternoon that rushes back upon my mind. The temporary platform on which he stood; the great black crowd; the languor of the sultry summer's day; the smell of the grass; the American twang in the preacher's voice; the text; the line of reasoning; the telling illustrations, and, above all, the passionate appeal, — these all come back upon me as I write. To me, at any rate, they are all inseparably associated with the picture of the Village Green. I said that I have seen this happen many and many a time. Aye, and not only in actual experience, but upon the pages of our best literature. How often, I wonder, did John Wesley preach on the Village Green? John Wesley brought about the greatest revival of religion in our history, and, according to Lecky, saved England from all the horrors of a terrible revolution. And this masterpiece of daring evangelism and sanctified statesmanship was accomplished very largely on the Village Green.

For the matter of that, every Village Green is crowded with preachers. For what is the green but so many millions of blades of grass? And what is more eloquent than a blade of grass? When God visited the earth amidst the dews of Creation's earliest morning, the first thing that awoke to greet Him was a blade of grass. Until then the earth was without form and void, and darkness was upon the face of the deep. Then God came! And the grass came! And the grass led out the new age. It was the first thing on the planet, and it will be the last. As soon as that first blade of grass peeped out upon a world uncultivated and unoccupied, it vowed that it would conquer and possess every mountain and valley, every continent and island, every inch of soil the wide world over! And it did! It sprang up everywhere. It spread a carpet for the feet of the living and a covering for the graves of the dead. We brush it back sometimes in order to build a house, or a city, or an empire, just as children sometimes keep back the tide for a while by building a brave castle with walls and outworks; but it is only for a while. The castle topples to pieces, and the water flows in; the empire crumbles at last; and the grasses wave proudly over the sites of fallen cities.

'We have covered many square miles of earth with buildings,' says Mr. Scammell, in his *Cheapside to Arcady,* 'and the birds look down on a province of grey instead of the beloved and familiar green. Six miles or more outward from the centre of London lies the boundary-line of the world of trees and grass; but we are surrounded and hemmed in by the sweet enemy, and nothing but the strenuous trampling of our millions of feet prevents the speedy reconquest of our city by the kingdom of vegetation. Some day the feet will be fewer and less strenuous; houses will fall and not be rebuilt; the tide of green will flow in, and that which was London shall be once more field and forest.' Casual passers-by regard the grass as an ephemeral thing, here to-day and gone to-morrow. But the wise know better. The old yew-trees there behind the church are a thousand years old; but the grass was there before the yew-trees sprouted, and the grass will still be there when the yew-trees are no more. If you bend your ear, you will hear a whispering among the grasses.

The grasses on the Green are always whispering. And there is a ripple of quiet laughter running through all that they say. It is the laughter of conquest.

Preachers of immortality are these deathless grasses on the Green. Did not Peter once draw a striking and dramatic analogy between the three most persistent things on the planet — the grass, the man, and the Word of the Lord? 'For all flesh,' he says, 'is as grass, and all the glory of man as the flower of grass. The grass withereth, and the flower thereof falleth away; but the Word of the Lord endureth for ever.'

The Grass! The Man! The Word!

These are the three most universal, immortal, invincible things on the face of the earth! The grass withers, and the petals of its flower blow away on the wind; yet it rises again and conquers everything! Man drops into the grave, and his glory is forgotten; yet, like the grass, he is everywhere, master of everything, the most godlike thing under the stars! But the Word outshines them both; for it never even fades or falls, never even dries or dies. 'It liveth and abideth for ever!' Year in and year out, it is as fresh and as sweet every morning as the dewy grass on the Green; and, age in and age out, its glory grows from more to more.

Crowded with preachers is the Village Green. Perhaps that is why George Eliot chose the Village Green as the scene of Dinah Morris's sermon. 'She stood with her left hand towards the descending sun, and leafy boughs screened her from its rays; but in this sober light the delicate colouring of her face seemed to gather a calm vividness, like flowers at evening. It was one of those faces that make one think of white flowers with light touches of colour on their pure petals. The eyes had no peculiar beauty, beyond that of expression; yet they looked so simple, so candid, so gravely loving, that no accusing scowl, no light sneer, could help melting away before their glance.'

Dinah spoke of John Wesley, whom she had heard preaching on a Village Green, and whom she, as a child, had imagined to be a special messenger sent down from heaven. As she gazed upon his finely chiselled face and pure white hair, and as she listened to his deep, rich voice and earnest speech, she had wondered if he would suddenly vanish and be caught up into heaven again!

And then Dinah spoke, as Wesley himself had spoken, of Jesus. 'The Son of Man is come to seek and to save that which is lost' — this was her text. With womanly winsomeness and womanly entreaty, she drew the hearts of the villagers towards her Saviour. Beneath the vast dome of St. Paul's or under the spreading branches of the elm-trees, it is a great and wonderful evangel; and we may very well leave the Village Green now that we have again caught the sweetness of that heavenly music.

VI - The Sieve

I WAS spending a few days at the spacious farmhouse that nestles under the shadow of Saddle Hill. It was getting towards evening. The boys had, one by one, sauntered in from the stables and the fields; the girls had returned from the byre. It was past tea-time; yet the evening meal stood untasted on the vast kitchen table. The snowy cloth was temptingly spread; piles of white scones and crisp oatcakes tantalized the appetite: the kettle sang merrily on the hob; and yet we waited. For my good hostess, the farmer's wife, had gone to town for a day's shopping, and had not yet returned.

'If she catches the five-twenty, she'll be home in ten minutes,' pleaded Jean, with a coaxing glance at her hungry brothers. 'Let's wait till then!'

And, surely enough, in a few minutes there was a sound of wheels, and the good woman came bustling in with her parcels. The daughters of the farm withdrew to their mother's room, primarily, of course, to help her off with her hat and coat, and, just incidentally, to have a peep at her purchases. And then, to the undisguised satisfaction of the boys, the family circle was completed, and the meal began. All went merrily until, in the very midst of our festivity, the chink of cups and the hum of conversation were suddenly interrupted by my hostess. In answer to a question from Bella, she threw herself back in her chair, lifted her hands in a gesture of amazement, and exclaimed:

'Why, I do declare, I forgot the very thing I went for. Oh dear, oh dear; I've got a head like a sieve!'

Now I spent so many delightful days under her hospitable roof that I am reluctant to subject her utterance to public criticism. And yet I cannot allow her unhappy metaphor to pass unchallenged. A memory like a sieve, indeed! No simile could be more false to fact. It is the essential property of a sieve to allow the fine sand to escape whilst retaining the larger nuggets. But did she not herself tell us that it was the important thing — the very thing she went for — that slipped her memory? That is characteristic of the memory. It is very rarely like a sieve. In ninety-nine cases out of a hundred it is the big things that elude it, whilst a conglomeration of trifles remains.

In one of his soliloquies the Poet at the Breakfast table tells how, an old man now, he distinctly remembers being cheated out of sixpence by an old strawberry-woman at an English fair fifty years ago. Yet a hundred matters of really first-class importance have failed, during that half -century, to make any lasting impression on his memory! 'What an odd thing memory is,' he exclaims, in telling the tale, 'to have kept such a triviality and to have lost so much that was invaluable! She is a crazy wench, that Mnemosyne; she throws her jewels out of the window, and locks up straws and old rags in her strong-box.' A man remembers the first fish that he ever caught long after many of the more vital events In his career have faded from his mind. With perfect clearness he will recall to his dying day the shining, scaly trout, flapping in its death-flurry on the green bank under the willows. The winning hit that a man once made for the school eleven lingers in his thoughts long after the twists and turns of his later history have passed into the obscurity of forget-fulness. The thrill of that glorious moment will rush back upon him in his last illness. These are the happenings that haunt the memory.

Perhaps the apparent discrepancy is due to our false estimate of things. It Is possible that the memory has a truer sense of proportion, a more just per-spective, than we are wont to suppose. An artist does not select his subject because of Its commercial value or historic importance. A rustic cottage may be much more attractive to his brush than a king's palace, a parliamentary building, or a stock exchange. Memory claims to be allowed to judge things, as the artist does, by standards of her own. I was talking one day to a friend of mine who, a few years ago, lost his sight. He was telling me that he re-members with singular vividness a walk that he once took from his native town in England to a neighbouring village. He was sent by his father with a most important message. But he has forgotten now what that message was. He only remembers a squirrel that he saw in a beech-tree down the lane along which his journey took him. Now my blind friend would, at the time, have regarded the business that took him along the lane as of very much greater moment than the squirrel he saw perched saucily in the beech-tree; but the memory has tossed to the scrap-heap the mission on which he trav-elled, whilst he sees the squirrel to-day as clearly as he saw it thirty years ago. And, on the whole, he is convinced that memory is right. The squirrel is the thing that is best worth remembering.

As I sit scribbling on this Australian verandah, and think of my own child-hood on the other side of the world, I find that the things that most easily rush back upon me are not the important things. I remember — oh, how clearly! — my first circus! I went up to the top of our street in the dinner-hour to see it enter the town! The elephants, the camels, the cages of wild beasts, and the huge triumphal cars! On one, at a height that made me dizzy as I looked up, sat Britannia, attended by a bevy of beautiful princesses; on another sat a haughty conqueror, surrounded by his officers and followed by his slaves. Here in the procession rode Red Indians in full war-paint, with moccasins and bowie knives. There were men of all kinds and colours; how could I ever forget the wonder of that tremendous moment? And then there was the day when, a small boy, I went to school as usual and was told on ar-rival that Mr. Farncombe, the old schoolmaster, was dead! Would I like to see him? I was afraid, and did not like to say so; at last stammered feebly a reluc-tant consent; and was led, with half a dozen other shrinking and terror-stricken youngsters, past the coffin in which our old master lay so frightfully stiff and still. Can I ever forget that weird, uncanny moment, or the strange, unearthly dreams of the night that followed? And then there was a day when there was some little commotion in the home. I forget what it was all about; I know that my mother was ill in bed, and sent to know the cause of all the hubbub. As a result, I remember that I was haled before her, charged with having done something or other of which, as it happened, I was entirely innocent.

'And did you do it?' my mother asked, looking up from her pillows.

'No, mother!' I answered.

'Then that's the end of it,' she said to the nurse who had me in charge. 'If he says he didn't, he didn't!'

I was set at liberty, and scampered away feeling that my mother was the sweetest creature that ever breathed, and thinking what a horrid thing it would be to deceive her.

These are the things that the memory treasures.

They do not seem to be the critical hours of a man's experience, the pivotal points on which his career turned. Life would have gone on in pretty much the same way if these things had never happened. And yet it may be, as I have suggested, that the memory has a more just standard of values than we sometimes think. Let me look at these things again. The day on which I saw the circus was the day on which a world-consciousness was born within my soul. I had read of elephants that crashed through African forests, and of camels that crossed Arabian deserts, and of tigers that haunted the jungles of Bengal. I had heard of conquering heroes, of tattooed savages, of feathered Indians, and of woolly-headed slaves! But here they all were! I was too excited to reflect that it was largely a matter of dye and drapery! To me it was the world! All the continents and islands had suddenly swept into my soul. In bewildering and overpowering pageantry, they burst upon me all in a moment! And my memory treasures not the objective cause, which was trifling, but the subjective effect, which was tremendous! And that ghostly scene at the old school! My memory clings to it as the occasion on which death and I first looked into each other's faces. And the incident in my mother's bedroom! It was the hour in which I learned the meaning of faith. My mother trusted me; believed me implicitly; and life seemed a greater, holier thing in consequence. Is it not possible that memory discriminates with extraordinary insight and wisdom? She knows what to hoard up and what to throw away. Like the artist, she has her own standard of values; and the more we examine that standard, the more we shall admire it. The little things she treasures so jealously are, more often than not, the biggest things in life after all!

Moreover, there is this to be said. The memory not only knows what to keep, but, having kept it, she knows where to find it, and how to use it, when the occasion at length arises. In *It is Never Too Late to Mend*, Charles Reade tells how a party of miners belonging to the gold-diggings in New South Wales went for a stroll one Sunday and came upon the settlement of a new immigrant who had brought out with him from England a caged lark. The savage men gathered round the cage, but the bird was strangely silent. 'And then the same sun that had warmed his little heart at home came glowing down on him here, and he gave music back for it more and more, till at last, amidst the breathless silence and the glistening eyes of the rough diggers hanging on his voice, out burst in this distant land his English song. Sometimes, when he paused, a loud sigh from many a rough bosom, many a wild and wicked heart, told how tight the listeners had held their breath to hear him; and when he swelled with song again, he seemed to every one of those rough men to be singing of the green meadows, the quiet brooks, the honey clover, and the English spring. Shaggy lips trembled, and more than one drop trickled from fierce, unbridled hearts down bronzed and rugged cheeks. For these shaggy men, full of oaths, and strifes, and cupidity, had strolled about the English fields with sisters and brothers, had seen the lark rise and had heard him sing this very song. Those old playmates lay in the churchyard, whilst they themselves were full of oaths, and drink, and lusts, and remorses; but, in this immortal song, no note was changed. And so, for a moment or two, years of vice rolled away like a dark cloud from the memory, and the past shone out in the song-shine. They came back, bright as the deathless notes that lighted them, those faded pictures and those fleeted days; the cottage; the old mother's tears when he left her without one grain of sorrow; the village church and its simple chimes; the clover-field hard-by in which he lay and gambolled while the lark praised God overhead; the chubby playmates that never grew to be wicked; the sweet hours of youth, and innocence, and home!'

When the treasure was stored away in the casket of memory, it was only the trill of a lark in the English fields; but, like pence that had been magically transformed into pounds, it became invested by the passing years with a deep significance and a spiritual value. Many of the really fundamental events in the lives of these Australian diggers the memory had tossed away. She had kept no record of them. But she had carefully treasured up the song of the lark and the vision of the English fields. And she knew why. Her discrimination is almost infallible. I wonder if any such thought entered into the mind of the Great Teacher when He spoke of laying up for ourselves treasures that no moth can corrupt, that no rust can defile, and that no thief can break through and steal?

Part Three

I – Slip!

The deck of an ocean-liner in a tropical sea is the laziest place on the planet. Nobody dreams of promenading. During the intervals between meals the deck-chairs are all occupied, and each chair is carefully adjusted to such an angle that the occupant is practically reduced to horizontality. Fancywork reposes peacefully on the laps of the ladies, and a few brave spirits keep up a pretence at reading. But the book, however exciting, fails to grip; and every now and again the hand collapses beneath its burden, whilst the eyelids involuntarily close. For the rest, we sprawl and doze and dream, and await the sounding of the next gong.

Henniker and I had just come up from afternoon tea. We sat down side by side and abandoned ourselves to the prevailing lethargy. I must have fallen asleep; for when I opened my eyes, the chair that Henniker had occupied was empty, and the Chief Engineer was approaching. He took the vacant seat, and, after a few preliminary inquiries and observations, began to talk about things in his own department. He was disappointed, it seemed, with the previous day's run. We had done three hundred and thirty knots; he thought it should have been three hundred and forty.

'Well,' I said, 'and how do you account for it?' 'Oh,' he replied, 'it can only be owing to slip.' I had to confess that the expression conveyed nothing to my mind, and he considerately proceeded to dispel my ignorance.

'Oh, well, you see,' he explained, 'all that we can do down in the engine-room is to see that a maximum of power is generated by the furnaces and communicated by the engines to the shaft. But a certain waste of energy takes place between the propeller and the water. It may be that a heavy sea lifts the screw into the air occasionally. Or it may be that the pitching of the vessel keeps the screw too much in the light water near the surface instead of in the heavier water deeper down. Or it may be that, for some other reason, the water does not offer the necessary resistance to the blades of the propeller. That waste of energy, however it occurs, we call *slip*. Yesterday, if the *slip* had been normal, we ought to have done three hundred and forty knots. As it is, we only did three hundred and thirty. The *slip* must have been more serious than we thought.'

Almost immediately he was called away. But as I sat there on the deck, with the empty chair at my side, I found that the information with which the Chief Engineer had supplied me provided food for a good deal of reflection. One has not to go to an ocean-liner in Mid-Atlantic in order to discover cases of *slip*. Accidents will happen in the best regulated families. Wherever there is a generation of energy, there is a greater or smaller escape of energy. Wherever there is power, there is *slip*. Indeed, in thinking it over since, I am convinced that my friend, the Chief Engineer, is less troubled by *slip* than most of us. His work is liable to *slip* at but one point — the point at which the propeller strikes the water — whilst the work of most of us is subject to *slip* at quite a number of points.

Take the artist, for example. He comes most readily to mind, because I have just left him. I was strolling along the beach this afternoon, enjoying the expanse of blue water to my right, the stretch of yellow sand before me, and the riot of green forestry extending to the horizon on my left. I clambered over a pile of rocks round which the waves were playing, and, under their shadow, came suddenly upon a painter busy at his easel. He was facing a massive bluff of red sandstone surmounted by a tangle of tea-tree and scrub. I entered into conversation with him, and was soon confirmed in my impression, that, in his case, *slip* may occur, not at one point, but at several. To begin with, however carefully he may scrutinize the great cliff in front of him, something of its ruggedness and beauty is sure to escape him. A greater artist would discover some gleam of light or shade that he fails to notice.

And with the greater artist it is only a matter of degree; he would observe more, but he would still miss something. Then, in the second place, there is a certain amount of *slip* in expression. My friend the artist confessed that he could never convey to his canvas all the beauty that he did see. The picture in his soul is always a little lovelier than the work upon the easel. And then, later on, there is a certain amount of *slip* in the eye of the admirer of the picture. For the picture is not for the painter; it is for the public. And the most appreciative observer never sees in the picture all that the artist sees in it. At these three points, therefore, there is *slip*. There is *slip* in the painter's observation of the subject treated; there is *slip* in his attempt to express on canvas the beauty that has charmed his eye; and there is *slip* in the perception of the spectator who afterwards gazes, however sympathetically, upon the painter's handiwork.

But I owe the artist an apology. I have pressed him into my service violently and at random. Like Jephthah's daughter, he was the first person I met in the course of my seaside cogitation of my theme; and I consequently seized upon him as my victim. But he will not, I hope, object to my stating that anybody else would have served my purpose just as well. It is true that nobody sees in the picture all that the painter puts there; but, then, the same principle holds true of every worker. Supposing, when I clambered over the boulders that projected into the surf, supposing that I had found, reclining in the shade on the other side, not an artist, but a statesman, or a musician, or an author, or a preacher. Either would have provided me with an equally welcome victim, and, like Jephthah, I should have hurried him off to my altar. For, however carefully the statesman expounds his proposals to the House, his scheme is never perfectly apprehended. A certain amount of *slip* occurs in his own exposition of his ideas; and a further element of *slip* characterizes the perception of his hearers; and so the policy that reaches their intelligences is little more than a shadow of the splendid project that stirs his soul to such enthusiasm. And as he listens to the damaging speeches of his opponents, and reads the adverse criticisms of the newspapers, he is tortured by the conviction that, to a very large extent, he has been misunderstood. It is a case of *slip*. It is the same with the musician. The most fervent admirers of Beethoven, or Wagner, or Chopin, or Handel, do not hear in the oratorio all the sublimities and profundities that swept the soul of the composer when first he committed his passion to paper. Only the author can perfectly appreciate a book. His writings must, of course, stand or fall by the judgment of others. It is his business, not only to think great thoughts, but skilfully to convey those thoughts to other minds. His fine conceptions will not excuse his faulty expressions. But for all that, the fact remains that the most brilliant writer cannot so arrange his language as to make it a perfect vehicle for his thought. Something is lost in communicating his meaning to his manuscript. And even the best of readers sometimes nods. All that the author thought is not written; and all that is written is not read; and so, at both stages, *slip* takes place. And if, resting on the sands, I had chanced upon a minister, I am certain that I should have found him a victim exactly to my taste.

For neither the artist, nor the statesman, nor the musician, nor the author is as much troubled by *slip* as the preacher. At the outset, the themes with which he deals are so sublime, so awful, so incomprehensible, that, in the nature of the case, his conception of them must be very partial and very inadequate. Then, like the statesman and the author, he is under the humiliating necessity of employing language as the medium of his thought. And it is a very imperfect medium. As Tennyson says:

...words, like Nature, half reveal
And half conceal the soul within.

Words — even if he always selects the best words — mean different things to different people, and convey different notions at different times. And then, again, he does not always select the best words. The man has never been born whose command of language amounted to absolute perfection; and, so far as it falls short of absolute perfection, he must perforce convey by his utterance something less or something more, or something other than his meaning. In spite of all oaths and affidavits, no man ever yet told the truth, the whole truth, and nothing but the truth. It is not in the power of mortals to do it. Let two men, transparently honest and scrupulously careful, tell of an experience which they have shared; and the tales will differ materially in the telling. The impression conveyed by the one will diverge at several points from the impression created by the other. Language being what it is, and the human mind being what it is, it is impossible to speak without unconsciously understating, or overstating, or falsely stating the case. A liberal quantity of *slip* must therefore characterize the attempt of the preacher to express to his hearers his own very imperfect conceptions. And what of the congregation? Even if all his conceptions were immaculate, and all his language faultless, he must still allow for a certain amount of *slip*. Between his own lips and the perceptions of his hearers there are innumerable avenues for the leakage of his energy. The acoustic properties of the building may not be perfect. The ears of the congregation may not be good. Sultry conditions or defective ventilation may induce drowsiness. And then, even at the best of times, thoughts are wayward things. Minds will wander. Even during the delivery of his most impassioned periods, the men will, in a flight of fancy, *slip* back to their offices; the mothers will be once more among the little ones at home; the young men and maidens will be dreaming romantically of each other. Everything is not heard; and, even if heard, everything is not fully comprehended. *Slip* occurs at every point.

The only remedy for this lies in sane and judicious repetition. It is the duty of the pulpit to say the same things over and over and over again. They must be clothed in different phraseology, and illumined by fresh illustration, and approached by a new line of thought; but the things that are really worth saying must be said repeatedly. Allowances must be made for *slip*. I remember that, some years ago, an idea laid hold of me with more than ordinary force. It was burning in my bones. I felt it my duty to give utterance to it at every possible opportunity. I took it into my pulpit, and stated it, as effectively as I possibly could, to my own people. A week or two later I was invited to speak at a Methodist anniversary. I delivered my soul again on the same theme; but I noticed in the audience one gentleman, a prominent citizen, and a man of considerable culture and devotion, whom I distinctly remembered to have seen in my own congregation when I first broached the theme. A week later I was under an engagement to address a large public meeting in the City Hall. I once more harked back to my old subject; and, to my horror, as I was speaking, I caught sight of the face of my former hearer. I felt ashamed to be saying the same things to him a third time. But I thought of the words, *'Jesus saith unto him the third time...'* and proceeded to state my case as forcibly as I knew how. At the close of the meeting, as I was leaving the hall, I found my friend waiting, and not to rebuke me. 'I was greatly impressed,' he said, 'by what you were saying to-night,' and he went on to tell me of what he himself proposed to do in the matter. He gave no hint of having heard me speak on the subject twice previously. Apparently I had then made no impression. Whether it was my fault or his is beside the question. The point is that *slip* takes place, and we must allow for it. *'Jesus saith unto him the third time'* — and so must we.

It may be that, one of these days, we shall discover that the *slip* of life is less than we fancied. We may find that the escaped energy, although it did not propel the ship, served some other useful purpose. Longfellow made some such discovery:

I shot an arrow into the air,
It fell to earth, I know not where;
For, so swiftly it flew, the sight
Could not follow it in its flight.

I breathed a song into the air.
It fell to earth, I know not where;
For who has sight so keen and strong
That it can follow the flight of song?

Long, long afterwards, in an oak
I found the arrow, still unbroke;
And the song, from beginning to end,
I found again in the heart of a friend.

Those who make such delightful discoveries may be left to enjoy their felicity undisturbed. But, since we are living in a world in which some arrows go astray and some songs fall flat, it is as well to take no risks. A wise man will allow for *slip*. Does the arrow appear to have missed its mark? He will draw the bow again. Does the song seem to have reached the heart of nobody? He will straightway tune his voice, like Browning's thrush, to sing a second time.

II - The Four Idols

We are all idolaters. It is in the blood. Race memory is a wonderful thing. Old Bruno lies sprawling there on the mat. The children can pull at his ears; the kittens can play with his tail. He takes no notice. He blinks and bears it. What is he dreaming about as he lies dozing there with his nose resting on his paws, the very picture of tameness and domesticity? Jack London says that a dog only has one dream. He is back in the forest primaeval. He is dreaming of the old wolf-days; the days when his ancestors were fierce and wild; the days when every mouthful of food was won by ripping and slashing, by the stern authority of tooth and fang. He is a wolf yet in the soul of him, a wolf with all his wolfishness under severe and galling restraint. And so, I say that, after the same fashion, we are all idolaters. We may not now worship Thor and Woden, Freya and Tyr, at least under those names; but we have our idols yet. Francis Bacon, in a passage which Macaulay regarded as among the very greatest and most influential contributions ever made to literature, charged us with worshipping four. And he named them. Beware, he said, beware of the Idols of the Tribe; beware of the Idols of the Cave; beware of the Idols of the Marketplace; beware of the Idols of the Theatre! Bacon was concerned with these counterfeit divinities as the enemies of pure reason, the foes of accurate thought, the perverters of sound judgment; but we need be bound by no such narrow limits.

I

There is the *Idol of the Tribe*. It is the contagion of the crowd; the tendency to applaud when the multitude applauds and to hiss when the people hiss; the disposition to do as everybody else does. A recent traveller speaks of a certain island upon which he came in the course of his voyagings. It was a perfect paradise. Its climate was of the softest; its vegetation the most luxurious; its flowers the most beautiful and fragrant; its birds of the most exquisite and gorgeous plumage. The inhabitants seemed, on first acquaintance, to be gentle and kindly. But, to his horror, he quickly discovered that the people cherished the most hideous and revolting superstitions, and practised the most frightful and abominable cruelties. No individual member of the tribe could defend these horrible proceedings. Indeed, each individual, consulted separately, condemned and deplored them. Each trembled lest he should himself one day fall a victim to their insatiable demands. Yet the thing went on!

It had always been so; it had never been challenged; everybody on the island submitted to it; nobody thought of questioning its continuance. Each was the victim of all, and, unwittingly and unwillingly, m each helped to tyrannize all! Here, then, is the Idol of the Tribe! One has not to go to the South Seas to find it.

Why do we dress as we do — one way this season and another way next season? Why do we dress one way; the Chinese in another way, and the Red Indians in still another way? Who ordains these arrangements, both as to general outline and particular style? We obey the Idol of the Tribe. Here are two brothers, Oliver and Godwin Peak, engaged in conversation. They are, of course, George Gissing's creations, but I may borrow them from *Born in Exile*. 'Oliver was going out; his silk hat, a hat of the very latest fashion, lay with his gloves upon the table.

'What is this thing?' inquired Godwin, with ominous calm, as he pointed to the piece of headgear.

'A hat, I suppose,' replied his brother.

'You mean to say you are going to wear that in the street?'

'And why not?'

'Can't you feel,' burst out Godwin, 'that it's a disgrace to buy and wear such a thing?'

'Disgrace! What's the matter with the hat? It's the fashionable shape!'

Godwin turned contemptuously away. But Oliver had been touched in a sensitive place, and was eager to defend himself.

'I can't see what you're finding fault with,' he exclaimed. *'Everybody wears this shape!'*

'Everybody!' replied Godwin, with withering disdain. 'Everybody. How you can offer such an excuse passes my comprehension. *Have you no self?* Are you made like this hat, on a pattern with a hundred thousand others?'

Now what in the world is this that we have unexpectedly discovered in listening to two brothers as they discuss the hat that lies upon the table? It is nothing less than a resurrection of the Baconian philosophy! For see!

'Everybody wears this shape!' pleads poor Oliver.

'Everybody! Have you no self?' demands the angry Godwin.

It is Godwin's way of charging his brother with being a worshipper of the Idol of the Tribe.

Now, if the Idol of the Tribe threw the baneful glamour of his superstition only over hats and gloves, skirts and blouses, nothing would have induced me to meddle with it. But, unfortunately, his spurious divinity aspires to preside over much more serious things. For, like mantles, morals are largely a matter of fashion. 'Succeeding generations,' says a great historian, 'change the fashion of their morals with the fashion of their hats and their coaches; take some other kind of wickedness under their patronage, and wonder at the depravity of their ancestors.' For centuries we tolerated slavery. The whole thing was fraught with anguish and shame. But then — everybody did it! And because everybody did it, no one troubled much about it. Each worshipped secretly the Idol of the Tribe.

I sometimes fancy that, even in our churches, the Idol of the Tribe is worshipped more often than we think. Here is a great evangelistic service! The hearts of men are strangely stirred. Each person feels that, if he were alone in the universe, he would become a Christian. But he is not alone. The place is crowded. The last hymn is sung. The people stream out into the street. There is chatter and laughter and noise. The sacred impressions are soon forgotten. Everybody does it. The Idol of the Tribe has secured his costliest oblation at the door of the sanctuary.

II

There is the *Idol of the Cave.* The cave is the home. There the man is monarch of all he surveys. An Englishman's home is his castle. In designing it, in constructing it, in furnishing it, he thinks of nothing but its comfort. He will make everything as congenial, as agreeable, as snug as it can possibly be made. And so far all is well; nobody can find fault with him. But our philosopher is afraid that he may carry his craze for comfort a little too far.

For a man is more than a mere cave-dweller. He has a mind; he has a heart; he has a soul! He needs not only things, but thoughts; not only furniture, but faith. He is a thinking animal, an emotional animal, a believing animal. Whether he means to do so or not, he will find himself providing himself with a small stock of convictions. He may do it deliberately and systematically; or he may do it casually and absent-mindedly; but he will do it. It is a race-habit. And the danger is that, unless he is very careful, he may select the articles of his faith on the same principle on which he selects the articles of his furniture. He will gather together a few agreeable conclusions; he will provide himself with a comfortable creed; he will fit himself out with a neat little stock of congenial beliefs; and then he will rub his hands, lie back at his ease, and congratulate himself on his shrewd discernment and excellent taste.

This is the Idol of the Cave. Beware of it! says Bacon. He would have me to know that I cannot select my conclusions as I select my chairs; I cannot pick and choose a few beliefs as I would pick and choose a few bedsteads. Bacon says that I should cultivate the habit of distrusting my agreeable conclusions. Whenever I find myself believing what it is pleasant to believe, I must carefully investigate the matter. It may be that I am worshipping the Idol of the Cave. It may be that I believe this thing just because it is nice to believe it. I am to suspect my agreeable conclusions. To suspect them; not necessarily to reject them. Bacon is too wise a guide to counsel me to reject a conclusion simply because it is so attractive. As a great Christian he knew as well as I do that some of the things that are most credible are the things that are most delightful. We believe them, and find it heaven to believe them. But we do not believe them because they are so captivating. Only a Stoic, an ascetic, a misanthrope, would ask me to reject a conclusion because it is so charming. To adopt such a course would be, not to worship the Idol of the Cave, but to fall prostrate before a still more hideous god. Bacon would never encourage such idolatry. Suspect your agreeable conclusions, he says. Do not reject them, but overhaul them. Analyse them; verify them; confirm them.

III

There is the *Idol of the Market-place.* The Market-place was a great place in Bacon's day. A world that knew nothing of our modern ways of advertisement and swift communication got over its difficulties by bringing everything to the Marketplace. And the Market-place is a good place. God has built His world very largely on a commercial basis. Barter and sale are the essence of life. The Market-place is for money-making; and there is nothing but good in the making of money as long as the money is made in the Market-place. The rivalries of commerce have sharpened the wits of the race. The desire of each man to provide a better article than his neighbour has prompted a hurricane of invention and discovery. 'There are,' says Dr. Alexander Mackennal, 'two services which wealth may render to society; the pursuit of it may make strenuous men; the employment of it may make generous men; he who tries to gain what he may liberally use will become both strong and noble through the discipline.' Here, then, is the sanction and glory of the Market-place.

But the making of money must be kept to the Market-place. That is the significance of the story of the Cleansing of the Temple. Jesus, we are told, 'went into the temple of God, and cast out all them that sold and bought in the temple, and overthrew the tables of the money-changers, and the seats of them that sold doves.' And why? Is it not good to buy and sell, to exchange coin, to offer doves for sale to those who need them? It is — *in the Marketplace!* But not in the Temple! Jesus was protesting against the commercialization of that which never ought to be commercialized. He was hurling out of the Temple the Idol of the Market-place.

This stone image of a god — is it a good thing or a bad thing? You say it is a bad thing. But was it a bad thing in the quarry? Is it bad, that is to say, in itself, or has it been made bad by the hands of bad men? These coins — are they good or bad? It depends on the use to which they are put. As soon as you introduce the commercial spirit into something outside the Market-place, you are in trouble. What about the commercialization of sport? Is not sport a good thing? But the introduction and rapid development of the professional spirit has largely been its undoing. Is it not a striking thing that the Puritans, who condemned almost every form of recreation and enjoyment, kept racehorses? Cromwell did. He thought that the matching of horse against horse was one of the most stimulating forms of enjoyment, and that the opportunity of meeting his friends on the turf was conducive alike to physical and intellectual recreation. What has reduced horse-racing from this high pinnacle to the plane on which it stands to-day? The answer is obvious. We have commercialized that which did not lend itself to commercialization. Or take politics. Are not politics a good thing? But when Sir Robert Walpole waves his hand towards the members of the House of Commons and exclaims, 'All these men have their price!' we feel that the lowest depth of degradation has been sounded. The thing has been commercialized. It is the worship of the Idol of the Market-place. As soon as you commercialize a good thing, whether it be a temple, a football-field, or a Parliament, you degrade it. As soon as you commercialize a bad thing, you perpetuate it. Could our fathers have borne so long with slavery, and could we have borne so long with the liquor evil, but for the vested interests involved? Beware, says Bacon, of the Idol of the Market-place.

IV

There is the *Idol of the Theatre.* Now to understand what Bacon means we must glance at the theatre as it existed in Bacon's day. The drama was then a very primitive affair; and among the most notable respects in which it differed from the drama of to-day stood the fact that there were no actresses. And why were there no actresses? Why were women prohibited from appearing upon the stage? Why were the feminine parts all played by boys? If we can solve that problem, we shall catch just that subtle element in Bacon's thought that led him to speak of the Idol of the Theatre. The fact is that those Elizabethan pioneers of the modern drama thought that women are naturally so sympathetic, so intense, so fervidly emotional, that the very process of projecting themselves in imagination into the personalities which, in their stage parts, they represented, would leave some permanent impress upon the individuality and character of the actress. They felt that women would become affected, tainted with unreality, and spoiled.

Beware, then, says our great English philosopher, beware of unreality! Does not the very word 'hypocrisy' mean 'the playing of a part'? It is essentially a stage word. Beware of the Idol of the Theatre! Once more our philosopher would apply the warning particularly to thought. Beware of pretending to accept conclusions that are not really your own. Beware of pretending to reject conclusions that, in your secret soul, you acknowledge! There are two kinds of hypocrites. There are the people who pretend to be a great deal better than they are; they are the minority. And there are those who pretend to be a great deal worse than they are; they are the majority. There are those who pretend to be Christians, and are not; and there are those who pretend not to be Christians, and are. Both are playing a part; they are indulging in an affectation; they are tainting their souls with unreality; they are guilty of hypocrisy. Bacon would urge both of them to give up their play-acting. Beware, he would say, of the Idol of the Theatre!

V

Miss Kingsley tells of a certain medicine-man in West Africa who found himself at death's door. He applied all his herbs and spells, and conducted all his well-worn rites before his idols without any effect. At last he wearied of his hocus-pocus, and took his idols and charms down to the sea-shore and flung them into the surf, and he said, 'Now I will be a man and meet my God alone!' The greatest hour in a man's life is the hour in which he spurns the Idol of the Tribe, the doing of what everybody does; the Idol of the Cave, the doing of what is agreeable to him; the Idol of the Market-place, the doing of what pays him best; and the Idol of the Theatre, the doing of that which does not reflect his real and genuine self; and stands an honest, sincere, and penitent idolater in the august Presence of the Holiest of All.

III - His Worship the Mayor

For many a long year Tammas Dalgleish was Mayor of Mosgiel, and reigned without a rival. At election after election the little old gentleman was returned unopposed. Indeed, it came to be regarded as the natural thing. Nobody quite knew why. I have a notion that it was just because Tammas was old. The other members of the Borough Council were aggressive young townsmen, the warmth of whose ardour incubated all kinds of municipal policies, and the restlessness of whose brains littered the council table with an infinite variety of schemes. The result was inevitable. As soon as Councillor MacDonald stated his policy, the council fell into two parts as though it had been cleft by a sword. Half the councillors said 'Hear, hear,' and half shook their heads sagaciously, and muttered to each other that it would never do. And when, a few weeks later, Councillor Campbell outlined his scheme, the council was once mxore rent in twain. Half the councillors supported; half opposed. The same fate befell each of the other councillors in turn. There was only One member of the council who never concocted a fresh policy or

93

formulated a new scheme. That was Tammas Dalgleish. His abstinence in that respect gave him an immense advantage when the mayoral election came round. Councillor MacDonald would have made an excellent Mayor, and his claims upon the honour were considerable; but then, he had a scheme! His elevation to the mayoral chair would place him in a position of commanding influence; it would invest him with a casting vote and other dangerous prerogatives; and it would probably lead to the adoption of his scheme. The hostile councillors said once more that this would never do. And so it came to pass that none of the councillors, save Tammas Dalgleish, could command a majority of votes when the elections came round. Year by year, therefore, as regularly as the second Saturday in November returned, it was announced from the verandah of the council-chambers that only one nomination had been received, and that Councillor Dalgleish had been declared elected for a further term. The little old gentleman beamed, expressed his sense of the honour that had been done him, and promised that he would endeavour to prove himself worthy of the confidence of the citizens. Which meant, being interpreted, that he promised to sink peacefully into the chair for another year, never daring to think out a policy himself, or even to say Yea or Nay to any of the troublesome schemes that the younger and noisieir councillors might present. It all passed off very pleasantly. There was speaking and cheering and drinking of healths. Everybody seemed perfectly satisfied with the turn things had taken. And certainly Tammas Dalgleish was.

He was an amiable little old man, not destitute of frailties. One of these was his excessive modesty. He was terribly afraid that we should forget either that he was a Scotsman, or that he was Mayor of Mosgiel. He had every reason to be proud of both these circumstances; and, as a matter of fact, there was not the slightest danger of our forgetting either; but he was obviously nervous about it. In the course of my twelve years at Mosgiel I came to know him pretty well, although only on two occasions did I have direct dealings with him. Of those two events I propose to tell the story now; and if into the first narrative there steals a suspicion of comedy, it will be seen that the second story is sufficiently dramatic to atone for that defect in its predecessor. But to my tale.

It was in the days of the South African War. When it was announced that Lord Kitchener was conferring with the Boer leaders at Pretoria, everybody felt that peace was not far off. This conviction fastened upon the mind of old Tammas Dalgleish, and he decided to call a meeting of citizens to arrange for a worthy celebration of the glad event — when it should come. He was good enough to call at the manse and ask me to be present. I very cheerfully consented. At the meeting, over which he presided, a programme was drawn up, a committee was appointed to carry it into effect, and, at His Worship's suggestion, I was appointed convener. We soon got things into shape and only awaited the declaration of peace to have everything moving. At last the welcome signal was given. The screaming of syrens, the ringing of bells, and the booming of guns apprised all and sundry that the war in South Africa had passed into history. I hurried down to the council-chambers, found His Worship there before me, and we soon got to work. The morning was occupied with the distribution of medals to all the children of the town. The main event of the day was timed for two o'clock. All the townspeople were asked to assemble at the junction of the main streets; led by the local band, they were to sing first the Doxology and then the National Anthem; and, after that, the procession was to start.

At two o'clock, however, rain was threatening. The outlook for the procession and the subsequent events was very gloomy. When I entered the council-chamber a few minutes before the hour, I found His Worship in a state of extreme tension. He was tortured by visions of trees being planted and foundation-stones laid under torrential skies.

'Come on,' he said impatiently, as I saluted him, 'let us get the procession away at once! What's to be done?'

'Very little, your Worship,' I replied, handing him a fresh copy of the programme. 'You have simply to ask the people to join in singing, to the music of the band, first the Doxology and then the National Anthem.'

I saw at once that he was displeased. He was for waving his hand and ordering the procession to start. I held out for the programme, the whole programme, and nothing but the programme.

'Well,' he exclaimed at last, in a more conciliatory tone, 'let us split the difference. Let us drop the Doxology and sing the National Anthem!'

I pointed out that the Doxology was singularly appropriate to the occasion; that it was specially decreed at the meeting of citizens; that it was on the printed programme; and that its omission would seriously wound the sentiments of many of the citizens.

His Worship lost all patience. I saw ten minutes later that he imagined the Doxology to be some ponderous kind of oratorio that might detain the procession for a good part of the afternoon. But I did not grasp his point of view until, looking daggers at me, he sprang up, rushed bareheaded on to the verandah, raised his hand to secure silence, called at the top of his voice, 'The band will lead the people in singing the Doxology,' and then added, with terrific emphasis, *'One verse only,'* In the years that followed, it was quite a common occurrence, when things were getting lively in the council chamber, for one of the councillors to suggest that they should sing together the second verse of the Doxology! And His Worship always smiled good-humouredly.

It happened, a year or two later, that Dr. Harry Grattan Guinness came to Dunedin and conducted a series of special meetings in the largest theatre there. I was unable to go into town to any of the earlier meetings, but I saw that the series was to conclude with a couple of illustrated lectures, one on South America and the other on the Congo. I promised myself at least one of these; and, on the night of the South American lecture, I set off for the city. The lecture and the pictures far exceeded my anticipations. I was delighted, and resolved to return next evening. On my way to the station the following evening, whom should I meet but His Worship the Mayor? To this hour I cannot tell why I suggested such a thing; but before I knew what I was saying I was inviting him to accompany me! He was the last man on earth whom you would think of inviting to a missionary lecture.

'You ought to come, sir,' I was saying. 'I went last night, and did not mean to go again; but the lecture was simply splendid, and the pictures were magnificent. I am sure you would enjoy it.'

Before I realized what had happened, he had accepted my invitation, and we were walking side by side on our way to the station. I spent most of the time in the train wondering by what strange impulse I had asked His Worship to accompany me. That riddle was still unread when we reached the theatre. It was filling fast. Surveying the crowd we noticed a couple of vacant seats about half-way up the area and slipped into them.

As on the previous evening, the lecture was most interesting, and the pictures were among the best of the kind that I have ever seen. For all practical purposes we had left New Zealand miles behind, and were in the wilds of Central Africa. An occasional side-glance at my companion told me that he was as interested as I was. Then, suddenly, a change came over the spirit of our dream.

'I propose now to show you,' said the lecturer, 'the photographs of some of the men who have laid down their lives upon the Congo.'

I was afraid that this purely missionary aspect of African life would possess less interest for His Worship, and I was prepared for yawns and other indications of boredom. The coloured pictures of African scenery gave place to the portrait of a fine young fellow in the prime of early manhood. To my inexpressible astonishment His Worship almost sprang from his seat, grasped the back of the chair in front of him, and stared at the screen with strained and terrible intensity.

'It's my boy!' he cried, loudly enough to be heard some distance away. 'It's my boy! It's my boy!'

I naturally supposed that he had been affected by some curious similarity of appearance. Fortunately his agitation had not been noticed from the platform, and the lecturer went on.

'This,' he said, 'is a young fellow named Dalgleish who came to us as an engineer to superintend the construction of our mission steamer...'

'It's my boy!' cried my companion, overcome now by uncontrollable emotion. 'It's my boy, my poor boy!'

Neither of us had eyes or ears for anything that followed. His Worship sat beside me, his face buried in his hands, swaying from side to side in silent agony. Every now and again he would start up, and I had the greatest difficulty in restraining him from rushing to the platform to ask more about his dead son. Sitting there beside him, it came back to me that he had once told me of a boy who ran away from home and went to London. 'We were too angry at the time to answer his letters,' he had said, 'and so, after awhile, he gave up writing, and we lost all trace of him.' When the great crowd melted away that night, I took His Worship to the lecturer's room, and introduced them to each other. The identity of the fallen missionary was established beyond all doubt, and Dr. Grattan Guinness arranged to come out to Mosgiel and spend the next day with the Mayor and his wife.

He did. I was not present, and I do not know what took place. But I often fancied, from little indications that I noticed afterwards, that the things that were said, and the tears that were shed, in the course of that visit were a means of grace to my friend, His Worship the Mayor.

IV - The Lantern in the Lane

The soul of the artist shone through his wrinkled face. I really believe that, had his great gift been encouraged and trained, he would have taken his place among our most eminent Australian painters. I shall never forget the last time I saw him. After a long drive across the plains and round the foot-hills we reached Wattle Glen just as dusk was falling. He and his wife — a gentle old lady, with a soft, musical voice, and hair as white as his own — came out to the car and insisted that we must stay the night. During the evening she took me into the front room and showed me the pictures he had painted since my previous visit.

'But he will never paint any more,' she said, with that subdued sadness with which very old people speak of increasing infirmities. 'His sight is failing fast. He only recognized you by your voice when I led him out to the car.'

As we rose, after an evening of pleasant reminiscence, to take our candles, a sweet and tearful smile played over her face, and, stepping towards me, she said:

'I must tell you a little secret. It is our Diamond Wedding-day. We were married just sixty years ago this morning. That is one reason why we were so delighted to see you, and so anxious for you to stay the night. We should like you to lead us in our thanksgiving.'

I blew out the candle and returned it to the table, taking instead the Family Bible that she handed to me. She turned with a flush of pride to the entry that was just sixty years old. I was deeply touched by being permitted to lead them in their worship on that memorable night; and when I rose, with the glow of the sacred exercise fresh upon my spirit, I had no desire to open fresh conversation. An immediate retirement seemed more in keeping with the eternal fitness of things. I turned to go. And then, to my surprise, the old gentleman broke the silence.

'Those were beautiful words that you read,' he said, 'about the light shining in a dark place; would you mind repeating them?'

I took the Bible and read again: *'We have also a more sure word of prophecy; whereunto ye do well that ye take heed, as unto a light that shineth in a dark place, until the day dawn and the day star arise in your hearts.'* He leaned forward, listening intently.

'Beautiful pictures!' he murmured, lying back in his chair, as though totally unconscious of our presence. 'Beautiful pictures! I have never painted anything like that!'

I

I took my candle and retired, puzzling over his words. And yet, when I looked at them again, I was surprised that I had never noticed the vivid artistic touches in those graphic phrases. The pictures sailed before my fancy now like a series of dissolving views. *'A dark place!' 'A light that shineth in a dark place!' 'The dawn!' 'The daystar!'* It is a perfect gallery of masterpieces!

'A dark place!' There rushes instantly to mind some tortuous track. It is hedged about by dense forestry; it winds and twists and forks and branches; the huge boughs overhead blot out the sky. The traveller who, with no light to shine upon his path, attempts to thrid this labyrinth, is in a pitiable plight indeed. He cannot see his hand before him! He stumbles over a gnarled root; he kicks against a heavy stone; he puts his foot into a hidden burrow; his face is torn by a straggling wisp of thorn. Sometimes the continuous crunching of the scrub beneath his feet tells him that he has left the track altogether. It is a dark place. It may be that Peter's picture suggested Dante's. Dante tells of the time when, at the age of thirty-five, he awoke to the fact that he was lost.

> In the midway of this our mortal life,
> I found me in a gloomy wood, astray,
> Gone from the path direct: and e'en to tell
> It were no easy task, how savage wild
> That forest, how robust and rough its growth.
> Which to remember only, my dismay
> Renews, in bitterness not far from death.

But where is this dark place, so vividly described first by Peter and then by Dante? Do they mean to say that *the world* is a dark place? And, if so, is it true? Is the world a dark place? Is it not bathed in brightness? Is it not the best of all possible worlds — a world that makes you glad to be alive? Can any man look upon a field of corn all flashing with red poppies; or upon a range of snowcapped mountains piercing the blue canopy above; or upon the sun sinking to rest in a tropical sea; or upon the waves dashing themselves into spray on a rock-bound coast; and declare, in spite of all this, that he is living in a dark place? Can any man who has ever gathered wild flowers in the lane; or who has made friends with the furry creatures of the woods; or who has marked the plumage of the birds out in the forest; or who has seen a salmon glitter as it comes flashing from the stream; can any such man say that the world is a dark place? Can a man watch the children romping on the village green; or listen to the song of the nightingale; or drink in one long liquid peal of laughter; or take part in the boisterous fun by the fireside, and say that the world is a dark place? When my old friend spoke admiringly of this picture, among others, on his Diamond Wedding-day, was *he* thinking that the world is a dark place? But let us jump to no hasty conclusions. Does Peter really say that the world is a dark place? Or does he merely affirm that the world would be a dark place *if it were not for the Bible?* This sure word of prophecy, he says, is like unto a lantern shining in an otherwise dark place, and, by its illumination, saving the place from its own darkness!

And perhaps that is a true description of the world after all. It *must* be true, or my old friend would not' have thought it so artistic. The world is *not* a dark place. At least, it is not a dark place *for us.* But it would be a very dark place for us if we had no Bible, no knowledge of God, no clear revelation of His love and care. And it is still a very dark place for those to whom these priceless blessings have not come. Take the savages, for example. Barbaric people live for the most part in climes where Nature is more prolific, more gorgeous, more luxurious, than in these temperate zones. And yet life under such conditions, so far from being a picnic, is a night-mare. The savage is surrounded by companions whom he cannot trust, and he feels himself to be at the mercy of natural forces of which he is horribly afraid. Every puff of wind that blows upon him is the breath of a demon. The air is full of hateful and malignant spirits. He knows not at what moment they may take it into their heads to destroy him. He lives in Paradise, but his Paradise is Purgatory to him. We know no such terrors. We have been taught that all these forces are under control. We have come to feel that they are governed by inscrutable wisdom, by unerring justice, by infinite love. We may or may not be decidedly Christian; but we have read our Bibles, or come under the influence of those who have. And the sacred revelation there made has banished all superstitious horrors. We are calm, restful, unafraid. The world is not dark, but delightful. Yet it is only delightful because of the lantern in the lane.

II

'Beautiful pictures!' murmured my old friend on his Diamond Wedding-day, sitting back in his chair and conjuring up before his sightless eyes the fair dreams that my reading had suggested. 'Beautiful pictures! I have never painted anything like that!'

The lane!

The lantern in the lane!

But my old friend saw a third picture. The dawn is breaking! The day-star is in the sky! As yet, it is true, the light is dim, crepuscular, uncertain. You are glad that you have the lantern in your hand. But, still, the darkness has gone! The grey dawn is filtering through the branches overhead; And, high above you, is the Morning Star! What did Peter mean, I wonder, by this third picture? He leaves us in no uncertainty. For see! '...a light that shineth in a dark place, until the day dawn and the day-star arise *in your hearts!*' It is the light breaking *within!* It is the dawn of Christian experience! In his *Horae Subsecivae* Dr. Brown comments on the picture of Luther in the Convent Library at Erfurt, and he lays stress on the fact that, as Luther pores over the sacred pages, the dawn comes stealing in through the windows. 'The young monk,' he says, 'is gazing into the open pages of a huge Latin Testament — we can see that he is reading the opening chapters of the Romans. A few dangling links indicate that the Bible was once chained — to be read but not possessed — it is now free and his own! Next moment he will come upon — or it on him — the light from heaven, shining out from the words "Therefore being justified by faith, we have peace with God," and, in intimation of this, His dawn, the sweet pearly light of morning, shining in at the now open lattice, is reflected from the page upon his keen, anxious face.' That is a touch of real spiritual genius. The imagery is unmistakable. The monk was reading the Bible in a dark place, when, suddenly, the day dawned, and the day-star arose in his heart!

The dawn! When the dawn comes stealing through the trees, the old lane becomes a new place. The branches are choral with song, and the air stirs with the hum of insect life. 'The day dawn from on high hath visited us!' sang the aged Zacharias when his lips were unsealed by the spirit of prophecy. He saw that the dawn had come, and that the old world was pulsing with a new and strange awakening. Yes, when the dawn comes stealing through the trees, the lane becomes a new place. In *With Christ at Sea* Frank Bullen has a great chapter entitled The Dawn.' It is the story of his conversion. And he tells how, having been led to faith in Christ by those majestic and inspired words that he had heard read to him by the seamen's missionary, the whole world seemed a new place to him. The leaves seemed greener, the sky bluer, the flowers sweeter. It was *'the dawn'*! To such a man the old lane is a dark place no longer! It is heaven upon earth! The dawn has broken! The day-star has arisen in his heart! His faith is fortified now by the strongest of all possible arguments — the argument of experience. The things that he has felt and known may not convince others; but they have lifted him beyond the reach of doubt.

III

And as I let my memory play about the look of triumph on my old friend's face that night, I am convinced that, among the pictures on which his blind eyes were so rapturously gazing, there was still another, and that other the brightest of them all. For is not the dawn the promise of the day? Is not the Morning Star the harbinger of the Sun himself! To be sure! If the exquisite symbolism of the apostle means anything, it means that those of us who have kept the track in the darkness by the help of the lantern — the light that shineth in a dark place — shall yet walk down the old lane amidst the splendours of noonday, our eyes enchanted by a riot of colour and our ears charmed by a festival of song. I never expect to visit Wattle Glen again in this life. And, even if I do, I shall find that its glory has departed. The old artist and his gentle companion no longer journey together there by lantern light. The vacant stare has passed for ever from his eyes. I may find their names engraved on a stone in the little God's-acre close to the church. But his artist soul feasts upon the beauty that is ineffable, and revels in the fadeless light of heaven's eternal noon.

V - The Holly-Tree

I KNOW a holly-tree, a grand old holly-tree. It may be that there are other holly-trees with leaves as green and berries as bright; but, if so, they are unknown to me. The holly-tree whose praises I am singing stands beside the lovely lawn of a fine old up-country residence; its leaves always look as though they had just been cleaned and varnished; and the brilliant berries are a dazzling riot of red.

I used to wonder why the birds are so fond of the holly-tree. They are no more comfortable among prickly leaves than I am; and everybody knows that the berries are not particularly palatable. But the other day Mr. J. W. Go f ton let me into the secret. The holly-tree is a sanctuary. 'The tree,' says Mr. Go f ton, 'sheds a great many of its leaves after the summer has set in. These remain on the ground in thick profusion, and so formidable are their hard and pointed spines to the feet of such birdhunters as the cat, the weasel, and the fox that these creatures dare not attempt to walk across them. Consequently the birds soon find out that they can secure immunity from danger in a holly-bush; and throughout the autumn and winter a vast number of sparrows, linnets, buntings, blackbirds, and some starlings spend their nights in peace and quiet among its branches.' It is pleasant enough to lounge on the lawn on a sunny autumn afternoon, and, amidst the trees that are strewing all the ground with russet and gold, to admire the old holly-tree in all its bravery of scarlet and green. But it is even more pleasant, when the darkness closes in, and we draw our chairs up to the fire, to reflect that, out there beside the lawn, a score or more of timid, shrinking, feathered things have found a peaceful sanctuary, secure from all their foes, under the kindly and powerful protection of the holly-tree.

Now the holly-tree is not alone in this. The law of sanctuary is written everywhere. You chase the mouse until the frightened creature dives into its hole, and you know that your task is hopeless. The tiny thing has found sanctuary. You hunt a rabbit till at last it vanishes into its burrow under the long gorse hedge. You can follow it no farther. It has found sanctuary. In his *Fields of France* Mr. Macdougall tells how, in the merry month of May, the stag defies its keenest pursuers. Among the picturesque fields and forests of Fontainebleau the hounds and huntsmen meet. The scent is found. The chase opens gaily. But soon the flying stag takes to the valleys. And there 'a beautiful fault frustrates the sport, for, thick as grass, the lily of the valley springs in all the brakes and shady places. The scent of the game will not lie across these miles of blossom. The huntsmen are in despair, and the deer, still deafened by the yelp of the hounds, beholds himself befriended by an ally more invincible than water or forest oak, by the sweet and innumerable white lilies that every May-time send the huntsmen home. Feeding among the fragrant flowers, the gazelle exults in delight and safety.' Far off up the valley the trembling creature hears the baying of the disappointed pack; but he has found a sanctuary amidst the perfume of the petals. Mr. Seton and Mr. Stewart White have both told of the way in which the hunted animals of the great African and American forests will fly for sanctuary to the camps of men. 'Every night,' says Mr. White, 'a fawn used to sleep outside my friend's tent, within a foot of his head. It was seeking protection from the wolves by which its mother had been killed.' This most attractive law pervades the whole of life. It is everywhere. I can find no stick or stone in the solar system upon which it is not engraved.

But are these furry and feathered things the only creatures in the universe that need a sanctuary? Surely not! Peep into the nursery or the playground, and you will see that, from our earliest infancy, we ourselves seek its beneficent protection. In every game there is a home or a base or a 'fen' or a 'barley' or a touching of wood — a sanctuary of some kind whereby the tired player may find respite from pursuit. And, later on, why do we love at times to creep away to some lonely wood or quiet field or solitary beach? Is it not that, after the din and the dust, we find in the very stillness a sanctuary? As Mr. Herbert Tucker sings:

A sanctuary within the woods I know —
    A sheltered glade by the glad blue o'erspread,
Close-set and tall the pine-trees round it grow;
    By their shed needles it is carpeted.
And to its gracious solitude I steal,
    When my vexed spirit feels the stress of things;
Like some hawk-harried bird that hides to heal
    Its bloodied plumes, and rest its weary wings.

Even within the wondrous mystery of my own complex nature, I am continually coming upon unexpected operations of that lovely law that I discovered among the branches of the holly-tree. What happens, for example, when I go to sleep? A man spends his day in toil and worry and anxiety. Then at night he throws himself upon his couch, and the most wonderful thing happens. He closes his eyes, and where is he? He has left his worries worlds behind. He has found sanctuary. Or a man hurts a limb. The pain reaches a certain point. But beyond that limit his anguish cannot go. The limb becomes numb. He finds sanctuary. Or in sudden fear or mental agony one loses consciousness. We faint. It is a way we have of leaving the difficulty behind for a while. We plunge into oblivion, and find sanctuary.

And then again, turning to the social side of life, what a beautiful sanctuary is home! When a man is tired and feels that the world is hard, he turns away from his tasks at sunset, and goes home. And when he turns that handle, and sets that door between himself and his cares, and loses himself in the love of a wife who worships him, and of children who clamber to his knee, he feels that he has found a sanctuary indeed. And what shall I say of friends? God made a beautiful thing when He made friendship. All day long we are on our guard. We keep people at arm's length. We set a watch upon our lips. We speak with reserve. But at last we meet a friend, one to whom the soul is knit as the soul of David was knit to the soul of Jonathan. Reserve is thrown to the winds. We have secrets no longer. We unbosom ourselves with freedom. In the abandon of perfect friendship the heart finds its sanctuary.

Or look in still another direction. Professor David Smith tells of a great lesson that he learned, as a young minister, from his old teacher and friend, the eminent Professor A. B. Bruce. 'He introduced me,' Professor Smith says, 'to my first charge; and that Sunday night, as we sat in my study, he said to me, "You will get no inspiration from your surroundings here; see that you seek it from your books." I remembered his counsel, and I found it good. The years which I spent in that quiet parish proved very profitable. Many an evening I would come home sick of petty jealousies, and fretted by trivial narrownesses, and would get into my study; and, behold, I was in a large and wealthy place and in the fellowship of the immortals. My study was the most sacred and wonderful place on earth to me. It was my refuge and my sanctuary.' My sanctuary, mark you! And it was probably with this reminiscence of his early ministerial days in mind that Professor Smith penned for us the following verses:

I bless Thee, Lord, that when my life
   Is as a troubled sea,
I have, remote from its rough strife,
   Harbours to shelter me.

I bless Thee for my home, where love
   Her sweet song ever sings,
And Peace spreads, like a nesting dove,
   Her gentle, brooding wings.

And for this chamber of desire.
   Where my dear books abide,
My constant friends that never tire.
   Teachers that never chide.

In my London days I used to turn aside sometimes from the bustle and turmoil of the city, and stand for a moment in the spacious quiet of St. Paul's Cathedral. How delectable that stillness seemed as one crept in from the roar and tumult outside! And scattered about the great interior, one always saw, seated here and there, several with whom the world had gone very hardly. There was a haggard expression in the face and a hunted look in the eye. They had turned into the sacred precincts for a moment's breathing-space. They had found sanctuary. It is but a picture and a parable of the Church universal. She offers shelter to the battered and the baffled and the brow-beaten throughout the wide, wide world.

Indeed, it may be said that the Church is not only a sanctuary herself, but she literally dots the world with sanctuaries. They spring up automatically wherever she goes. They respond to her message as the flowers respond to the spring. What are your hospitals but sanctuaries for the diseased, the damaged, and the broken? What are your asylums, your infirmaries, your orphanages, your almshouses, your whole network of benevolent and philanthropic enterprise, but so many sanctuaries to which the distracted, the aged, and the unfortunate may repair? Like the fairy who transformed all that she touched into silver, Christianity, by some subtle magic of spiritual alchemy, turns everything that it touches into sanctuary. See how it laid its hands upon the heart of our own great empire, and turned every inch of our soil, and every ship on our seas, into a sanctuary for the slave.

Slaves cannot breathe in England: if their lungs
Receive our air, that moment they are free;
They touch our country, and their shackles fall.

'No matter,' said the eloquent John Philpot Curran, 'no matter with what solemnities he may have been offered upon the altar of slavery, the moment he touches the sacred soil of Britain, the altar and the god sink together in the dust, and he stands redeemed, regenerated, disenthralled.'

But, as is the case with so many subjects, the greatest word ever spoken about sanctuaries was uttered by one of those old Hebrew prophets who always seem to probe to the inmost heart of everything. *'A glorious high throne,'* he says, *'is the place of our sanctuary.'* A throne, a sanctuary! It seems self -contradictory. And yet, when you come to think of it, the throne is ever the best sanctuary. Sir Walter Scott has outlined this great truth for us in the tender story of Jennie Deans. She was tempted to save her wayward sister by a lie. It was a very little lie, a mere glossing over of the actual truth. The slightest deviation from actual veracity, and her sister's life, which was dearer to her than her own, would be saved from the scaffold, and her family honour would be vindicated. But Jeanie could not, and would not, believe that a lie could afford a real refuge. And she told the truth, the whole truth, and nothing but the truth. And then she set out for London. Along the great white road she trudged, until her feet were bleeding and her exhausted form could scarcely drag itself along the dreadful miles. But on she pressed, until she saw the lights of London town; and still on, overcoming every barrier, until she stood before the Queen. And then she pleaded, as no mere advocate could plead, for Effie. With what passion, what entreaties, what tears, did she besiege the throne! And, before the tempest of her grief and eloquence, the Queen yielded completely, and gave her her sister's life. That is the glory of the gospel. It is the introduction of the shuddering soul to the Highest Tribunal. And there, at the Throne, in the august Presence of the Highest, the stricken heart finds its solace, its satisfaction, and its sanctuary. It is as when the linnets cluster together on the smooth bark of the great holly branches, knowing that a thousand leafy spear-points protect them from all prowling beasts of prey. It is as when the hunted, terrified, and breathless deer enters the leafy glade to which the hunters cannot come. The soul that seeks the Throne has found sanctuary, true sanctuary, at last.

VI - Rifts of Blue

We do not see the stars in the daytime. They are there at noon just as much as at night, but the dazzling splendour of the sun shames them into invisibility. Something very similar occurs in the touching narrative of the sorrow at Bethany. It is the only story of a personal bereavement, told with vivid domestic detail, that the New Testament gives us. It closes sensationally with the raising of Lazarus. Sometimes I wish that it did not. That stupendous miracle has engrossed all our attention to the detriment of several exquisitely beautiful things that occur elsewhere in the story. The sun has blotted out the stars. I am going to forget for a few minutes the dramatic close of the story. I am going to read it again just as I would read any other record of domestic grief. And, reading it thus, I feel like one who, looking upward, gazes upon a sky overspread with grey and gloomy clouds, yet who sees here and there the most glorious rifts of blue. Those rifts of blue are openings into immensity, peeps into infinity, windows that open upon the everlasting. Let me point to one or two.

In the course of His journey to the stricken home Jesus said a very striking thing. 'Our friend Lazarus sleepeth.' Each word deserves to be examined under a microscope. To begin with, is it not intensely suggestive that, with Jesus, Lazarus is still Lazarus? He speaks of him still by the fond, familiar name, and by that name, in the thrilling climax, again addresses him. 'Lazarus, come forth!' And to that name Lazarus responds.

Where wert thou, brother, those four days?
There lives no record of reply,
Which telling what it is to die
Had surely added praise to praise.

105

We do not know. But wherever he was, he was still Lazarus. Death had done nothing to impair his own identity. He was still Lazarus in the thought of Jesus. He was still Lazarus in his own consciousness. By the old name Jesus called him. To the old name he answered. The grave robbed him of nothing that was really worth preserving.

II

Lazarus is still Lazarus; the old identity is unimpaired. Lazarus is still our *friend* Lazarus; the sweet old relationships are undisturbed. And best of all, Lazarus is still ours. '*Our* friend Lazarus.' If that means anything, it means that those whom we have loved long since and lost awhile are still our own. '*Our* friend sleepeth.' God does not toy with our holiest affections, giving us one day those whom He would have us love, and the next day taking them from us. Our own are our own for ever. Lazarus, though dead, is still *our* Lazarus. The same idea occurs in the Old Testament. In the first chapter of the Book of Job, which Carlyle considered the greatest drama ever written, we are told how Job, by one fell stroke of dire calamity, lost all that he had. And then, in the last chapter, we are told that 'the Lord gave Job twice as much as he had before.' And in each case there is an inventory. Job lost seven thousand sheep; at the end he possesses fourteen thousand — twice as many. He lost three thousand camels; six thousand are at last given him — twice as many. He loses five hundred yoke of oxen; in the last chapter he owns a thousand — twice as many. He loses seven sons and three daughters; in the last chapter seven sons and three daughters are born to him. Why are the numbers of sheep, camels, and oxen doubled, whilst the number of sons and of daughters remains the same? And since the number of sons and of daughters remains the same, how can it be said that he had twice as many as before? The reply is obvious. He had lost his sheep and camels and oxen *for ever.* His sons and daughters who had passed from his sight, together with the sons and daughters around his knees, gave him twice as many as he had before. It means that Lazarus is still our Lazarus. That is Wordsworth's idea in 'We are Seven.'

'Sisters and brothers, little maid,
  How many may you be?'
'How many? Seven in all,' she said.
  And wondering looked at me.

'And where are they? I pray you tell.'
  She answered, 'Seven are we;
And two of us at Conway dwell.
  And two are gone to sea.

'Two of us in the churchyard lie,
    My sister and my brother;
And, in the churchyard cottage, I
    Dwell near them with my mother.'

It appeared to her questioner that there was matter here for subtraction, but the curly-headed little maiden would not hear of it.

'How many are you, then,' said I,
    'If they two are in heaven?'
Quick was the little maid's reply,
    'O master! we are seven.'

'But they are dead; those two are dead!
    Their spirits are in heaven!'

'Twas throwing words away; for still
The little maid would have her will,
    And said, 'Nay, we are seven!'

She clung to her conviction that Lazarus is still our Lazarus, and she had the divinest authority for her simple faith.

III

Or, turning our faces in a fresh direction, let us peer through another rift in this leaden sky into the clear heavens beyond. Is it not very singular that on His arrival at the home in Bethany — *His* home at Bethany — He wept? In our bereavements we attempt to stifle sorrow by the thought of *their* happiness whom we have lost. Jesus knew intimately the perfect felicity of Lazarus, and yet He wept! He knew, too, that, in an hour, the joy of Mary and of Martha would be complete, and yet He wept! Do these tears need explanation?

It is, at any rate, a comfort that He wept. By weeping He at least assured us that there is nothing faithless, nothing wicked, in our tears. And it would be like Him to sympathize with us in our sorrow, however needless that sorrow might be. Sorrow is sorrow, even though there be no sufficient cause for grief; and, just because the anguish was there, He shared its bitterness. There is a lovely letter written by Mrs. Carlyle to that rugged old husband of hers in the course of which she tells him how, during a recent illness, she was greatly comforted by her maid. The girl only came into the room, and rubbed her cheek against her mistress's; but it strangely soothed her. 'And sometimes,' adds Mrs. Carlyle, 'I could tell that her cheek was wet, and her tears meant much to me.' I like to think of poor Jane Carlyle's letter when I read the story of those tears at Bethany.

And was there not an element of pity in them? Pity for the sisters, since they were unable to see all that He had seen — the glory upon which, with unveiled face, Lazarus was gazing; and pity for Lazarus too. He Himself knew what it was to leave that brighter world for this less radiant one, and He felt for Lazarus in having to make the same great sacrifice. Professor David Smith, in writing on the epistles of Isidore, "the Greek scholar and saint, quotes from a letter which Isidore wrote to Theodosius the Presbyter on this very matter. Isidore, says the Professor, was a gentle and gracious soul who had quitted the city of Alexandria and sought retirement that he might give himself to devotion and study. He had no aptitude for ecclesiastical activities and contentions, and his name never appears in the bitter and futile controversies which mark the Church history of that period; yet he exercised in his seclusion a rare ministry of rich and far-reaching beneficence. He was a scholar, and he was gifted with an understanding heart and a sympathetic spirit. Troubled folk turned to him in their perplexities, and they found in him a wise counsellor. He wrote letters near and far, and over two thousand of these have survived. In one he deals with this question as to why our Lord wept by the grave of Lazarus. 'Why,' he asks, 'did Jesus weep for Lazarus, knowing that He would raise him from the dead?' Isidore answers his own question. 'It was precisely on that account,' he says, 'that Jesus wept. Lazarus had entered into his felicity, and Jesus wept at having to recall him. The miracle was necessary in order to convince the unbelieving Jews of His divine title; but in His eyes, knowing as He did the eternal realities, it was a cruel necessity. The storm-tossed mariner had reached the haven, and He must call him back to the billows; the warrior had won his crown, and He must call him back to the conflict. And therefore He wept — not because Lazarus had passed into the joy unspeakable, but because he must return to this poor troubled life.' From any point of view, then, those silent tears are wondrously and divinely significant.

IV

Just one more rift in those grey skies. We have walked with Him along the Bethany road; we have sat with Him in the house of sorrow; let us, without waiting to witness the actual miracle, go with Him to the tomb. 'And He cried with *a loud voice,* Lazarus, come forth!' Why with a loud voice, since Lazarus lay at His feet? Old Matthew Henry, with rare insight, declares that He cried with a loud voice to show that He was not addressing the dead body at all. Had he spoken softly it might have been supposed that the living soul and the dead body were inextricably intermingled. He looked away from the dead body, and cried with a loud voice that it might be seen that He was addressing a living soul at a distance, and not a dead man close at hand.

And why was it needful to call upon Lazarus *by name?* There were no others lying in that grave. Would it not have been sufficient had He simply cried, 'Come forth!'? 'He singles out Lazarus by name,' says Augustine finely, 'lest all the hosts of the dead should hear His voice and come forth together!' The time had not yet come for that. Some day He will say, 'Come forth!' and the dead will rise from land and sea at His sublime behest. But on that day at Bethany He only wanted one. He named His man, and, from out the world invisible, Lazarus instantly came at His call.

V

Peering through these rifts of blue, I clearly see two things. I see that, wherever those old companions are whom I have loved long since and lost awhile, they are within *His* care and at *His* call. At any moment He has but to speak their names and they instantly rise to greet Him. And the other thing is this. He calls Lazarus, and Lazarus alone! Why only Lazarus? H it is in His power to summon our dear ones from their graves and restore them to their old familiar places, why does He not do it? The fact that He calls Lazarus, and Lazarus alone, proves indisputably that the others are better where they are. Wherefore comfort one another with these words.

VII - A Divided Diaconate

It is part of the poignant pathos of a minister's life that the good old men who, as his first officers, fathered him in his callow youth, fall into their honoured graves before he is well launched upon his long career. Like the pilot who steers the vessel through the narrow and treacherous channel to the harbour's mouth, and is dropped as soon as the ship is once tossing on the open sea, those revered fathers in Israel leave the young minister as soon as the initial difficulties have been safely surmounted. I confess that, as the years have multiplied behind me, I have felt an ever-increasing longing to go back, just for once, to the queer old vestry in which my first deacons were wont to assemble, and to find myself once more surrounded by those rugged old stalwarts, grizzled and grey, who welcomed me to Mosgiel nearly a quarter of a century ago. I looked into their faces for the first time as I stepped from the train at the end of my long, long journey from London to that little New Zealand township. They were standing, the centre of a large and excited multitude, on the railway platform in the moonlight; and nobody thought of shaking hands with me until those solemn elders had approached and gravely welcomed me. How my heart quailed that night as I gazed into their venerable faces! How ridiculously young and inexperienced I felt! But I soon discovered that behind countenances that were like granite cliffs there lay a great wealth of human tenderness. They pitied my loneliness, for had they not each of them crossed the same wide seas in the days of long ago? And, deep down in their hearts, I think that each man felt that I had come to bury him, and the thought brought a new softness into all their breasts. During the twelve years that I spent at Mosgiel they, one by one, slipped silently away. I was their first minister, and they were my first deacons. I dare say that the

Mosgiel church has been excellently served by its officers since then; but no group of faces assembled in that vestry could look to me like the apostolic successors of the old men of whom I am thinking to-day.

Of the brave battles that were fought in that old vestry I could, if I would, tell a stirring tale. The congregation had no idea that such tremendous debates ever took place.

'It's our practice,' Wullie explained to me at the first meeting I ever attended, 'it's our practice always to lay a matter unanimously before the kirk. The minority never says a word after we leave this room.'

And so it came to pass that no echo of the great debates held in that vestry ever reached the church meetings. At the larger assembly it was always my duty to announce that the deacons recommended that certain courses of action be pursued, and the matter passed without discussion. As a rule the faces of the men who had made up the minority at the earlier meetings were a study at such moments; but only the chairman had the opportunity of surveying those lightning-flashes and thunderclouds. Only once did the argument in the vestry become so heated as to be worthy of classification as a quarrel; and, as it has proved my only experience of the kind, I have promised myself the satisfaction of seeing it placed on permanent record.

It was Gavin — surnames were regarded as a redundance among these men — who made the proposal that led to all the trouble. Gavin was severely practical. He had a keen eye for the cutting of the hedges, the weeding of the paths, the painting of the buildings, and all that kind of thing. A most useful man was Gavin. He was absolutely innocent of any aestheticism; his one criterion of church music was its volume; he fairly squirmed under a quotation from Dante or Browning. I always associate Gavin with a certain annual church meeting. In order to lure the settlers and their wives from the distant farms and homesteads, it was our custom to supplement the annual business meeting with a coffee supper. On this particular occasion the strategy had been more than usually successful; the place was crowded, and the business had simply romped through. The evening was quite young when the end of the agenda was reached.

'Before I ask the ladies to bring in the coffee,' I said, 'is there any other matter with which we must deal?'

'Yes,' cried Gavin, springing to his feet, 'there is! We ought to have some rules drawn up concerning the lending of church property. Now there are those urns. They are lent to all the organizations connected with the church for their socials and soirees, and the members borrow them for weddings and house-warmings. And nobody cares how they are returned, or whether they are put back clean. Now, this very afternoon, when I came down to see that everything was in readiness for to-night's supper, I found half an inch of maggots in those urns!'

It was a most incisive and telling speech from his own point of view, but a perceptible gloom fell upon the coffee supper. It was happy for Gavin that the election of officers was over. Had it followed that speech, the ladies who had been busy over the refreshments all the afternoon would have voted against him to a man.

But to come back to the quarrel. It was Tammas who led the opposition. Tammas was our treasurer, and the man who got church money out of Tammas was regarded in the light of a genius. I can see him now, a massive old man of flinty and wrinkled countenance, with an odd way of looking searchingly at you over his spectacles. I should have been frightened of Tammas, but he tore all fear out of my heart on the night of my induction. I arrived in Mosgiel on a Thursday night; the induction took place on Friday. When it was all over, and the visiting ministers had departed, Gavin, Tammas, and I found ourselves standing at the gate together.

'And have ye no coat?' asked Tammas, in surprise.

'Oh, no,' I answered airily. 'I didn't think I should need it,' and I reached out my hand to say good-night.

To my astonishment the old man took off his own and insisted on my wearing it. If anybody saw me on my way home, they must have wondered what horrible disease could have reduced me from the bulk that I boasted when that coat was made for me, to the modest dimensions that I possessed that night.

A great theologian was Tammas. As soon as I announced my text, Tammas took a huge note-book from his breast-pocket and a stubby blue pencil from his waistcoat. On Monday morning Tammas would be at the manse door looking as though, in the night, the church had been burned down or the treasury pilfered. When the study door had shut us in, he would very deliberately unbutton the big breast-pocket and draw out the ponderous note-book with its terrible blue records.

The unthinkable glory of God,' he would read, holding the book close to his face; and then, looking severely at me, 'You spoke yesterday of the unthinkable glory of God.'

'Did I, Tammas?' I replied timidly, fearful of prematurely committing myself.

'You did,' he would say. 'Ye ken I took it doon at the time.'

Then, out from another of his immense pockets, came a well-worn Bible. And, from a list already prepared and drawn up in the note-book, he read passage after passage to show that the word 'unthinkable' was improper and misleading.

After I had committed old Tammas to his grave, I felt a little ashamed of the manoeuvre by which I circumvented this habit of his.

'I can see how it is, Tammas,' I said to him one Monday morning, when his criticisms had been a little more searching than usual. 'This all comes of trying to preach without a manuscript. I have not had sufficient experience to enable me always to use the precise theological term, and the consequence is I fall back on the second-best, or even an inaccurate one. I begin to see the wisdom of reading the sermon. Such blemishes as these would be less likely to occur.'

I knew that a manuscript in the pulpit was poor Tammas's pet aversion; and, surely enough, the old man came on Monday morning no more.

I shall never forget the meeting at which Gavin and Tammas came to high words. The scheme that Gavin introduced that night was one that he had cogitated for months. He had worked it out to the last detail. He had plans and specifications and estimates, and, as he enlarged upon his proposals, a look of fond pride came into his eyes. He already saw in vision the realization of his dream, and his soul was fired with admiration and affection. He sat back at last, leaving the plans spread out on the table.

Tammas slightly inclined his head and looked at Gavin over his spectacles — always an ominous sign. Then he slowly unbuttoned his coat and drew out the note-book that we all dreaded. He laid it on the table and very deliberately turned over the pages. Then he plied poor Gavin with a fusillade of questions. To make a long story short, he resisted the proposal on two grounds, the one financial, the other theological. Gavin had given no indication as to the sources of revenue from which he expected to meet the proposed expenditure, and he, as treasurer, would never consent to apply the offerings of the congregation to such a purpose. And then, taking out his Bible and consulting his blue notes, he proved from a text in the Prophet Amos and another in the Epistle of James that the suggestion was an outrage on revealed religion. I never saw Gavin more ardent nor Tammas more determined. The position looked to me particularly ugly. In the course of the discussion that followed, some sharp exchanges took place. Gavin gave it as his deliberate opinion that the church finances had drifted into the hands of a niggardly old skinflint, who could find a text or two to prove anything that suited him; and Tammas painted in lurid colours the doom of those stewards who squandered their Lord's money and brought wild-cat schemes into the house of the Lord. At last the proposal was defeated by a single vote. Gavin rose in anger, stuffed the plans hastily into his pocket, and strode out of the vestry. I noticed, however, that, in his wrath, he had forgotten his hat, which still reposed under the seat that its owner had just forsaken. I knew Gavin well enough to feel sure that he would not march home bareheaded.

We concluded the business of the evening about twenty minutes later, and followed Gavin out into the dark. The church lay a good distance back from the road, and a number of ornamental trees adorned the open space in front. As we walked up the path through this shrubbery, Davie, the youngest of them all, walked beside me and commented on Gavin's unseemly exit. I was on my guard, remembering the hat that, from my coign of vantage in front of them, I had seen under the vacated seat. I resolved to sound a note of warning.

'Oh, yes,' I said to Davie, but in a voice loud enough for them all to hear, 'but we needn't worry about Gavin; he's all right! He thinks about this church all day and dreams about it all night. He was here before you and I ever heard of the church, and I expect he'll still be here after you and I have left it!'

'I'm hearing all that ye say!' exclaimed Gavin, emerging somewhat shame-facedly from among the shrubs, and walking off towards the church for his hat.

It was a trifling circumstance, but I could tell from the tone of Gavin's voice that a work of grace was proceeding in his soul, and perhaps the incident paved the way for what followed.

I went to bed that night like a man whose bubbles had all burst, whose dreams had all been shattered. I was excited and dejected and miserable. It was a" long time before I could get to sleep; but when I did I must have slept very soundly. I awoke with a start, conscious of a light in the room, of voices in the hall, and of my wife — a bride of but -three months — in slippers and dressing-gown bending over me.

'It's Gavin and Tammas,' she explained, 'and they say they want to see you.'

'Why, what time is it?' I asked, rubbing my eyes in astonishment.

'It's twenty to one!' replied she.

'We want to see ye terrible particular!' cried a voice from the hall.

I nodded consent to their admission, and in they came, looking, I thought, extremely penitent. Gavin held out his hand, and, as he came nearer to the light, I saw something glisten in his eyes.

This is no the way we meant to treat ye the necht ye arrived,' he said, and he pressed my hand again. Tammas also approached.

'Ye must think as weel as ye can of us,' he said, as he too took my hand. 'We shall need all yer patience and all yer luv, and ye must aye teach us better ways. Gavin and I have arranged all about yon plans, and we shall easily fix all that up at the next meeting. Now ye must put up a wee bit prayer for us!'

I crept out of bed and knelt down beside Gavin. Tammas and the mistress of the manse were kneeling on the opposite side of the bed. If the utterance of lowly and contrite hearts is specially pleasing at the Throne of Grace, that must have been a prayer-meeting of singular efficacy and acceptance. Even Tammas wiped his spectacles when he rose. Gavin took his arm to help him along the dark path to the gate, and so ended my first and last experience of diaconal strife.

VIII - When the Tide Turns

There is always a vague sensation of sadness in watching the sunset; but the particular sunset of which I am now thinking was the last sunset of the year. And it had, therefore, a pathos of its own. It was a typical Australian midsummer evening. After tea I had left the house for a quiet stroll, and, lured on and on by the tempting twists of the tortuous track, I had wandered farther than I had intended. I came suddenly to the riverside, and noticed that the tide was right out. Before commencing the return I sat down on some heavy driftwood that the winter floods had flung into the shingly cove, and watched the violet and gold die out of the clouds over the mountain. When the last flicker of light had vanished I rose to go. How silent it all was! The very river seemed asleep! Everything seemed wrapped in the stillness of death — for was not the old year dying? A water-rat leapt from the bank into the stream, and swam round and round for a moment, describing graceful little circles on the smooth surface of the water. At other times I had been impressed by the silence of its movements; but, breaking up that uncanny hush, the tiny creature seemed strangely turbulent and noisy. The swimmer crept back to his home in the bank, and everything was quiet again.

But I had not gone more than a hundred yards before I was again startled. Not far away, out on the murky waters, lay a cluster of old hulks and barges moored in the sluggish stream. A strange flutter and commotion suddenly disturbed these slumbering craft. Such a tossing and jostling and swinging and bumping! Such a rattling of chains and creaking of timbers and straining of cables! What could it mean? I soon saw. It was the new tide surging up the river, agitating the old barges and breaking their repose. It was both a para-ble and a rebuke. The old is always stirred to fresh life and activity at the ad-vent of the new. Who is more excited than the grandparents when a new ba-by is born? I stood corrected. I had been lamenting the passing of the old year. I had forgotten that the house is hushed for a birth as well as for a death. The silence was the silence of eternity, the silence out of which new worlds rush into being. What cause had I for gloom? I was losing nothing; I was gaining everything! The heaving of the waters had opened my eyes; I was disillusioned! I felt that I must greet the unseen with a cheer, and went home with a smile of welcome for the New Year.

For the hubbub and commotion out in the stream when the tide came surg-ing in seemed symbolic of the eternal and pitiful feud between novelty and antiquity. I wonder if I can recall and record what it was that the surging wa-ters and the drowsy craft said to each other as their quarrel broke the silence of that lovely summer's night?

'Get out of the way!' cried the tide, as it pushed the old barges this way and that way, and seemed to be laughing at their slow movements and obvious infirmity. 'Get out of the way! We can't have the whole place littered up by the things of a past generation!' And it jostled them rudely and irreverently against each other.

Silly young tide! What good can it hope to do in the world except by means of these old barges? Let it lift them gently, bear them patiently, and make it possible for them to visit creeks and inlets which they could never enter at low water! These weatherbeaten hulks that the tide treats with such disdain represent the one means placed at its disposal by which it may render the world some real service before it ebbs and goes again!

'Oh dear! oh dear!' cry the sleepy old craft. 'What a nuisance it is! We were sleeping so peacefully; and everything was so still that even the splash of the water-rat startled us! And then there comes all this flutter and commotion!' And anybody who caught the testy tones in which the old barges muttered this remonstrance could feel how deeply they resented the coming of the new tide.

Silly old barges! For deep down in their dark and cavernous holds there were lying bags and bales and casks and crates that could never reach their destination at low water; and the new tide, as it came rushing, swelling, surging in, represented the one chance they had of getting their cargoes into port.

It is very sad and pitiful, this wrangle between the old barges and the new tide. It is always sad and pitiful and humiliating when we fail to recognize that the old and the new belong to each other, and that neither is complete without the other. It is the peculiar temptation of youth to treat the traditions of the past with impatience. And it is the special frailty of old people that they look with suspicion upon everything new. Youth always has its face to the future and worships the new. Age always has its face to the past and treasures the old.

Now about all this Jesus once said a very striking thing, which I blush to confess that I never understood until yesterday. 'Every scribe,' He said, 'who is instructed unto the kingdom of heaven is like unto a man that is an householder, which bringeth forth out of his treasure things new and old.' Things new and old, mark you! Not a jumble of new things and old things all mixed up together, like new wine in old bottles. But things that are, at one and the same time, both old and new. For no really good thing is either old or new. It is both. Bring me the most antique object you can find, and I will show you how startlingly new it is! Bring me the most newfangled idea that has come to light, and I will astonish you by revealing its hoary antiquity.

The wise householder to whom our Lord referred was, it always seems to me, Mrs. Wildman, of Mablethorpe. We all remember the passage in Lord Tennyson's *Life* of his father — the laureate. That lovely entry always fascinates me. It occurs in one of the poet's letters to his sweetheart, Emily Selwood. 'I am housed,' he says, 'with an old friend of mine, who, with his wife, is a perfectly honest Methodist. When I came I asked her after the news, and she replied, "Why, Mr. Tennyson, there is only one piece of news that I know, that Christ died for all men." And I said to her, "That is *old* news, and good news, and *new* news!"' *New and old!* The good woman was so instructed unto the kingdom of God that she brought forth out of her treasures things that were both new and old!

The old is so new! What is the oldest thing of which you can think? 'Old as the hills!' you say. Very well; and as the phrase falls from your lips my thoughts fly back to the grand old mountain over whose towering head and massive shoulders I watched the sun set only yesterday — the mountain 'with its head in the clouds and its feet in the sea.' How often have I wandered about its leafy tracks and wooded slopes! I can see it from my window as I write. Look at the scars up there on the summit — eloquent witnesses to wounds inflicted before our little race began. What cataclysmic changes the old mountain-peak has seen! What titanic forces tore those slopes in ages long gone by! What storms and earthquakes and glaciers! See these huge gashes, these precipitous cliffs, these beetling crags, these jagged ridges, these scarped pinnacles, these piled and broken boulders! Bring a geologist, and he will tell you wondrous tales of Ice Ages and Stone Ages, of Tertiary periods and post-Tertiary periods, as he reads for you these stony records.

Yes; here is antiquity with a vengeance. And yet, as I look out of my window morning by morning, it is not the antiquity, but the novelty, of the mountain that startles me. We look out upon its pointed peak when we rise, and flatter ourselves that, from its appearance, we can forecast the weather of the coming day. However that may be, one thing is certain. The mountain, like the divine mercy, is 'new every morning.' It is as fresh as the dew on the grass. It is never twice the same. One day it is wrapped in angry storm-clouds, majestic and terrible. The next it is sullen and dismal, gloomy and grey. Sometimes it appears blue and close at hand. Sometimes it looks brown and far away. Now it is gay and sunlit. Soon it will be snow-capped and glittering. And in winter it will wear a robe of radiant whiteness. But in any case it is always fresh. Each time we say, 'Well, we never saw it quite like that before!' And if we ascend its bushy slopes, and cultivate its more intimate acquaintance, it is still the novelty of this antique mass that astonishes us. Like some incorrigible coquette, the old mountain seems to take endless pains to renew its youth. It is true that here and there, in falling trees and fading grasses, there are signs of decay. But beside the prostrate blue-gum are a hundred supple young saplings, and the faded fern is already almost hidden by a dozen fresh young fronds. And so the mountain-side seems always to be wearing a fresh garb. 'Just look here!' cries one child, as she rushes back excitedly from her rambles; and 'See what I've found!' exclaims another. The mountain bewilders and embarrasses us by its very wealth of novelties. So new is the old.

And how ancient is the new! What is the newest thing of which you can think? A baby just born? When does a baby begin to be born? A baby is a very antique affair. All generations, right away back to Adam, slumber in this little child of yours. This newborn babe is about the oldest thing living. It is the natural emblem of antiquity. Sir Oliver Lodge, in a recent article, has shown how old our startling modern inventions really are. It is a simple matter of movement, he says. A man takes six old things and puts them in a fresh relationship to each other, and then calls the result a new invention. Volta, for example, took zinc, which is as old as the hills, and copper, which is as old as the hills, and acid, which is as old as the hills, and the three put together proved a sensational and epoch-making invention. What was there new about it? It was literally as old as the planet. And yet it was so new that it changed the face of the modern world, revolutionizing all our commerce, and turning our industries into new channels. Yes, all these old things are wonderfully new, and all these new things are wonderfully old! Antiquity and novelty are twin sisters.

Yes, they are twin-sisters, and, as is so often the case with twin-sisters, they grow into each other's ways and become interdependent. They need each other, and we need them both. If we had the new without the old we should be instantly reduced to imbecility. I can tell the difference between chalk and cheese because old experiences of chalk and cheese come to my aid. I recognize a tree as a tree, and a man as a man, because all the trees and all the men from out of my past rise up to help me. A newborn baby is in such a helpless condition of mental vacuity simply because he is so pitiably past-less. He has no chalk and cheese, no men and no trees, by which he can test and compare the bewildering objects that swim into his vision.

Similarly, if we had the old without the new we should be reduced to mental stagnation and spiritual paralysis. No man can live on old experiences. I need new mercies every morning, just as much as I need new meals. I need new visions, new ideals, new unfoldings of the Father's face, new applications of the Saviour's blood, new illuminations of the heavenly Spirit. Even though I move along the old routine, teaching the same old class, or preaching from the same old pulpit, I need new throbbings and pulsations of spiritual power.

Listen to the water-mill, all the livelong day!
How the clicking of the wheels wears the hours away!
Languidly the autumn winds stir the greenwood leaves;
From the hills the reapers sing, binding up their sheaves;
And a proverb o'er my mind like a spell is cast;
'The mill will never grind with the water that is past.'

However old the mill may be, the stream that turns it must be newer than the newest sensation!

www.ingramcontent.com/pod-product-compliance
Lightning Source LLC
Chambersburg PA
CBHW051839040426
42447CB00006B/606